Side by Side

Also by Jo Lamble & Sue Morris:
Motherhood: Making it work for you

Side by Side

How to think differently about your relationship

Jo Lamble & Sue Morris

FINCH PUBLISHING
SYDNEY

Side by Side: How to think differently about your relationship

This edition first published in 2000 in Australia and New Zealand
by Finch Publishing Pty Limited, ABN 49 057 285 248,
P O Box 120, Lane Cove, NSW 1595, Australia.

03 02 01 00   7 6 5 4 3 2 1

National Library of Australia
Cataloguing-in-Publication entry

Lamble, Jo.
    Side by side: how to think differently about your relationship.

    Bibliography. Includes index. ISBN 1 876451 09 2.
    1. Man-woman relationships. 2. Interpersonal relations.
    I. Morris, Sue. II. Title.

306.872

Edited by Sarah Baker
Text designed and typeset by *DiAgn* in Slimbach
Cover design by *DiAgn*
Editorial assistance from Ella Martin
Cover photograph from Austral International
Index by Carolyn Conlon
Printed by Southwood Press

Notes   The 'Notes' section at the back of this book contains useful additional
information and references to quoted material in the text. Each reference is linked
to the text by its relevant page number and an identifying line entry.

Photo credits   David Hancock (page vii); Dave Lovelace (p. 28); Pete Waeron
(p. 130); Christian Wright (p. 147, family photo).

Photographs   The photographs in this book have been included to illustrate
everyday moments in the lives of people, past and present. However, the people
featured in these photographs are not connected with stories which appear in this
book.

Contents

About this book

Our main aim with this book was to introduce the strategies we give to the individuals and couples who come to see us for help with their relationships. Our approach to successful relationships is making sure that both partners are responsible for themselves at all levels within their relationship. Gone are the days when couple counselling focused on teaching ways to communicate to your partner what they need to change in order for you to feel happier. It's up to you to look inwards and see what you can change in yourself, which will in turn have a positive effect on your relationship.

In *Side by Side*, we are talking about committed, lifelong relationships – whether you are married, in a de facto relationship, or in a blended family. We often use the terms 'marriage' and 'committed relationship' interchangeably. Gay and lesbian couples will also benefit from the strategies outlined in this book.

Our ideas have been collected from a variety of sources, including our individual clients, our colleagues, family and friends, and from many people who completed a questionnaire about relationships. Each chapter is made up of a number of different layers. There are quotes from those interviewed, input from our training as clinical psychologists, and techniques and exercises based on the psychological treatment model known as Cognitive Behaviour Therapy, developed by A. Beck and A. Ellis.

Throughout the book you will find exercises that require your input. The exercises are to help you apply the strategies to your own relationship. We want you to start thinking, talking and changing. In this time of increasing relationship breakdown, it is worthwhile thinking about how **you** can better your relationship. No relationship is perfect, but there is always room for improvement.

If you are reading *Side by Side* following the breakdown of your relationship, it might help you gain some insight into what went wrong. Whether you initiated the separation or not, there are lessons to be learnt. We hope that some of the strategies we suggest will help you to feel stronger and empower you to move on.

You could be looking for some premarital advice, trying to keep your relationship on track, or wanting help to cope after your relationship has ended. Whatever the reason, we hope you benefit from reading *Side by Side*.

Jo Lamble and Sue Morris

Before I ask my partner to change,
I need to look inwards and ask myself:
What can I do differently?

CHAPTER 1

Is your relationship working for you?

Elizabeth explained why she had come for help.

I feel my marriage is about to fall apart; I don't want it to, but I think it might unless something changes soon. I think my husband and I clash more now than we ever did. I don't feel he respects me and everything he does annoys me. I think I still love him, but after thirteen years of marriage, it's time somebody did something about it.

Most people in happy relationships will no doubt tell you that being in a relationship is good for them. Unfortunately, we don't have to look far to see the effects of broken relationships. So at what point does a happy relationship become a not so happy relationship, and then an unhappy relationship? Elizabeth was aware that she and her partner needed to do something about their 'not so happy marriage' – but what?

First,x Elizabeth needed to figure out which aspects of her relationship weren't working for her. Many people realise things aren't right, but are not sure exactly what is wrong. This is where counselling can be of great benefit. Second, Elizabeth had to decide how she was going to involve her partner in the process of change.

When people marry, or enter committed relationships by choice, they would probably say that being with that person is where they want to be. It's that simple. It would be rare to find someone who, in the beginning, expects to leave their relationship at some point down the track. From what we hear, it seems that over the past decade the number of people marrying has decreased, the number of people entering de facto relationships has increased, and the divorce rate has increased. Furthermore, people are marrying later in life and remarrying later still.

The question most people want answered is: *What changes to erode those feelings of happiness in a relationship?* For every couple the answer will be different. We want you to start thinking about any problem areas in your relationship, or potential triggers to problems. We strongly recommend that prevention is better than cure. If you are contemplating marriage or a committed relationship, then the best investment you can make is to attend some kind of premarital counselling. Such counselling can address potential problem areas in a structured way.

Side by Side is designed to help people at various stages of their relationship. First you are in the bubble of new love where the outside world is shut out and all you care about is your relationship. After the bubble pops, you slowly let in the outside world, and start making plans for the future. Ideally, you then enter into a mature relationship with love, intimacy and commitment. This mature relationship needs to survive ups and downs and, of course, the ruts. Many sections of this book will apply to everyone, and others will only apply to some of you. The main aims of *Side by Side* are therefore to:

- provide basic relationship advice (premarital onwards)
- help you understand and make an informed decision about commitment
- help keep your expectations of marriage realistic
- help identify problems you might be experiencing

@ provide you with strategies to improve a stale relationship, or

@ help you cope if a relationship has broken down

Let's start with our conclusions

We'd like to give you our conclusions up front so that you can keep them in mind as you read through the parts of the book that interest you. We have developed these conclusions from our work with individuals and couples, from personal experience and from the experience of our friends and families.

There are five important conclusions we want you to keep in mind:

1. Without commitment, a relationship is doomed.
2. A relationship is about walking side by side along the same path.
3. Thinking clearly is everything.
4. It's up to you.
5. There is no perfect relationship.

Let's look at these conclusions in a little more detail before we start focusing on specific relationships.

Without commitment, a relationship is doomed

Ever wondered which comes first, the chicken or the egg? Well, if the chicken were a successful relationship and the egg were commitment, the answer is clear – the egg comes first. Without commitment, there is no foundation for a relationship. Without commitment, there is no incentive to try everything you possibly can to make yours a successful relationship. Without commitment, it is too easy to leave or be unfaithful.

Given that commitment is the first step on the path to a successful relationship, it goes without saying that the decision to commit should not be taken too lightly. That is why we are such strong advocates for premarital counselling. Making an informed decision about commitment reduces the likelihood of unrealistic expectations and regrets.

Commitment is a mindset, a way of thinking that gets played out in everyday life. It goes something like this: *You are the person I choose. No matter what difficulties we face, either as a couple or as individuals, I will be there for you. My behaviour will reflect the fact that I have chosen to be in a relationship with you for the rest of my life.*

If you think about this idea for a moment, you can see that a stale marriage is no excuse for leaving. Being in a rut is one of the many problems you will face as a couple from time to time. Commitment drives you to make things better. This mindset steers you away from the temptation of getting close to someone else.

With this mindset in place, the other conclusions follow. Without both parties being committed to the relationship, you can try every strategy in this book and still never be in a happy relationship.

A relationship is about walking side by side along the same path

The important words here are **side by side**. We do not say that you walk 'as one' along the same path. That's because we do not believe that when two people commit to each other, they become 'as one'. The mindset of commitment involves being there **for** someone, not **as** someone. You are in a relationship **with** someone, you do not **become** someone.

The path along which you walk changes course many times during a relationship. The direction the path takes depends on what happens to you as individuals and as a couple. At some point, one of you might take the lead. The other follows because of the commitment you share. At another point, the path swings the other way because of what's happening for the other partner.

Once again, you are side by side. The experiences you face provide many challenges. A relationship's success is partly determined by its ability to accommodate change.

Any change will be handled more easily if you and your partner work as a team. As we say later, you can't be a team player if you're competing for points. If there is competition over the direction of the path, then the team is threatened. Two people working against each other weaken the relationship.

While we strongly encourage couples to adopt a team approach, it is of course essential to live your own life within a committed relationship. Looking after your own needs enhances your individuality and provides you with the personal strength for supporting your partner when necessary. Not living your own life leads to a lowering of your self-esteem which, in turn, reduces your capacity to be an equal player.

Thinking clearly is everything

How you think directly affects the way you feel and what you do. Often you do not need to change what is happening in order to feel better. By changing the way you think, a situation may trigger a less intense reaction.

The way you deal with situations is greatly influenced by your expectations. Your expectations are based not only on your experience, but also on your family history. Often the way in which you were raised can exert a strong influence on you as an adult, even if you are not aware of it.

Unrealistic expectations of marriage can set you up for failure. Unfortunately, these unrealistic expectations can lead to one or both of you giving up on the relationship. The solution is to change your thinking so that your expectations fall more in line with reality.

Our theoretical framework for *Side by Side* is the Cognitive and Behavioural Model of psychology. In this book, we call it 'clear thinking'. The model is based on the premise that in order to feel better, you need to change the thoughts that **cause** a negative feeling or reaction. For example, resentment, anger and jealousy are common negative feelings in relationships. In order to lessen the intensity and frequency of these feelings, you need to change the unhelpful thoughts that cause them. We will show you how to rework your thinking in this way later.

It's up to you

When you have a problem, you'll probably work out what you are doing wrong and try to fix it yourself, or you'll get help. When you and your partner are having problems, however, the chances are you'll blame one another and wait for each other to change. This blaming and waiting has a very destructive effect on the relationship. Each of you needs to take responsibility for the problem and look for the solutions. Being committed allows you to examine your own behaviour to see what changes can be made. Changing even a small part of **your** behaviour can have a very positive effect on your relationship. We call this the 'positive domino effect'.

In the past, couple counselling tended to focus on you telling your partner what they could change to please you. Modern counselling focuses far more on what you can change in **your** behaviour, which will in turn aid the relationship.

So owning your problems, instead of blaming your partner, is liberating. It means that you don't have to rely on anyone else to make you feel better. You can start this process by yourself. Similarly, owning your problems allows you to pick your fights. Looking inwards first can stop the knee jerk reaction that results in you attacking your partner because **you** are upset about something they did or didn't do.

We outline many strategies to help you look at how you can make yourself feel better, which will in turn benefit the relationship. We sum up these strategies in our OCEAN model of communication (see Chapter 9). It provides an easy guide to tackling both the simplest and the most difficult issues.

There is no perfect relationship

It all comes back to your expectations again. At the end of the day, there is no perfect relationship, so don't expect it. The aim is to be as happy as you can be and to bring out the best in each other, by being together. Acceptance and tolerance are more easily achieved if you are not striving for perfection. Major problems can be overcome. It is even possible to rebuild a relationship after an affair *if commitment is established*.

Once you drop the idea of striving for perfection, relationships can be a lot more enjoyable. We finish the book with some suggestions to help you achieve contentment, happiness and satisfaction within your relationship.

Telltale signs of trouble

There are always signs that a relationship is in trouble. Unfortunately, they often go unnoticed. If you recognise one or more of these signs, don't panic; just be aware you need to work on your relationship.

Some telltale signs include:

- decreased desire to spend time together
- withdrawing physically and emotionally
- increased arguments about problems (see the 'Common relationship problems' list following)
- decreased desire to confront issues, which results in avoidance and builds resentment
- decreased ability to resolve issues satisfactorily
- reduced sexual desire (which cannot be explained by other circumstances)
- fewer positive remarks to each other
- increased criticism of behaviour or personality, especially in public
- thinking about or threatening to end the relationship
- breaking up and getting back together
- talking to friends and family about relationship difficulties
- speaking nastily to each other

Common relationship problems

- different views about money
- sexual issues
- feeling misunderstood by partner
- lack of common goals
- difficulty in openly expressing opinions
- difficulty in expressing love and affection
- power struggles
- different views about parenting
- different interests
- opposing religious views

Money is a real problem area for us. He's super conservative when it comes to spending. We're comfortable and I am certainly not a big spender, but you'd think so by the way he carries on. It feels very much like he's the boss and what he says goes. I resent that.

Frances, 41 years

No matter what I do, it never seems good enough. She's never happy.

Jeff, 37 years

We often end up fighting about the kids. I think he is very critical of what I do with them, but it's easy for him when he's been at work all day.

Thea, 35 years

I have asked him repeatedly over the years to talk to me more about his work. I chat non-stop about mine. It doesn't seem to sink in and I often feel excluded.

Kate, 32 years

How content are you?

Now that we have given you our conclusions and outlined some potential trouble spots, it is worth stopping to assess your level of contentment and commitment. This assessment should be kept in mind as you read *Side by Side*.

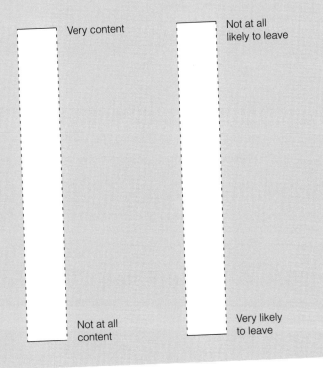

Barometer of contentment and commitment
In general, how content are you in your relationship at the moment? How likely is it that you would ever leave your relationship? On the first barometer below imagine you drew a line which best described how content you are. On the second barometer, imagine you drew a line which best described how likely it would be that you would leave.

Very content

Not at all
likely to leave

Not at all
content

Very likely
to leave

Where you would place the lines on these barometers is a useful indicator of where you should focus your attention. If you are not as content as you would like to be, then you can follow our many suggestions for improving your level of contentment. If you think there is a chance that you would leave your relationship, then you have some serious work to do on becoming committed because a relationship without commitment is doomed. If you are very content in your relationship and think there is no likelihood that you will leave, then your relationship seems to have a good chance of success.

IN BRIEF...

@ Without commitment, a relationship is doomed.

@ A relationship is about walking side by side along the same path.

@ Thinking clearly is everything.

@ It's up to you.

@ There is no perfect relationship.

Side by side

As we have just said in the first chapter, a relationship is about walking *side by side* along the *same path*. By making a commitment to someone, you are ***choosing*** to walk on that path together, regardless of the difficulties you may encounter along the way.

Your relationship path will be different to everybody else's. The direction the path takes will be determined by both of you. There will be twists and turns as well as really rough patches. Commitment enables you to follow the path, even if you did not choose its direction. Staying on the path together requires hard work and learning how to make difficult decisions. We hope *Side by Side* will give you some strategies to help make the going easier.

> **All relationships follow a path. It's how you walk the path that counts in the end.**

Two people do not become one

We talk about walking side by side along the relationship path, not walking 'as one'. When you commit yourself to another person, *you do not become 'as one'* with that person. This is something that may be hard for some people to swallow. What tends to be forgotten is that you have always been, and need to continue to be, two individuals – with your own thoughts, feelings and behaviours. Maintaining your individuality and uniqueness is an important step in ensuring you stay on the same path with your partner. If you lose the sense of who you are, resentment can easily build.

Who you are depends on how you were raised and on your life experience. You can't possibly expect the effects of such strong influences to disappear so that you can **merge** yourself with another. The belief that, when you marry 'two become as one', can easily lead to codependency, jealousy and shaky confidence. These, in turn, undermine the stability of a relationship.

> **For your relationship to succeed, it is important that you maintain your individuality.**

If individuality is lost, then you rely on your partner to meet your needs. For your partner to fully meet your needs, they would have to be solely focused on you, learn how to read your mind, and not do anything for themselves. Who wouldn't tire of this arrangement pretty quickly? Melanie's story highlights how becoming 'one' can spell trouble in a relationship.

Melanie's story (48 years)

I met Alan at university. We dated for three years before we got engaged. My family had never been close and I left home at an early age because of all the tension. Alan was so affectionate. It was wonderful. He was very close to his mum and dad who had a very happy marriage.

After we married, we kept working hard in our jobs, but spent every other moment together. I was worried that we would grow apart if we didn't share everything. I let go of my own hobbies and neglected my friendships.

When Alan had an affair and then left me, I was devastated, but above all, shocked. How could our marriage, which had been so close, fail? In couple counselling, Alan told me that he had become more and more uncomfortable with my dependence on him. I was just trying to have common interests! He also said that, several months earlier, he had noticed that he no longer found me attractive. He finally said that he didn't love me any more and that there was no hope for our marriage. We stopped going to counselling after that. There was no point.

Some of you, while reading Melanie's story, will nod your head knowingly. They were never going to make it, we hear you saying. Others will be wondering what is wrong with someone trying to have common interests and goals? To this latter group, we would answer, *nothing* – except, where did Melanie go? What happened to that individual who, before she met Alan, had had her own interests and goals? What happened was that she had worked hard at trying to become one half of a whole and, in doing so, lost her sense of self.

No doubt Alan also helped to create this exclusive unit. Initially, Alan probably saw Melanie's willingness to do the things he liked as a real positive in their relationship. In their case, it was Alan who first felt the discomfort of such dependency. It could easily have been Melanie. To illustrate what happens as a result of living out this fantasy of wanting to be as one, we can use the following model.

Why two people can't become one

1. The assumption that two people *should* become one causes one person to become passive, more and more eager to please, and self-sacrificing.
2. The other partner begins to lose respect for the passive person, finding them less attractive, and fails to speak up.
3. This loss of attraction and respect can lead to a lack of commitment to the relationship.
4. The passive partner tries harder to please and demands more reassurance.
5. The other partner withdraws further (because they see more of what they don't like) and becomes vulnerable to having an affair.
6. This partner shuts down and no longer makes any effort to work on the relationship.
7. Marital breakdown is likely.

How can you prevent this cycle occurring? We could say that had Alan spoken up at step 2, the relationship might have had a better chance of surviving. If counselling had been sought along the way, it might also have had a better chance. The important principle underlying this model is that you should both maintain your individuality. Ensuring that you maintain who you are as a person in your own right is vital to the success of your relationship. Remember who you were before you met each other, because that was the person who attracted your partner in the first place.

In Melanie and Alan's case, it is clear that Melanie began to lose herself and therefore her self-esteem. A loss of self-esteem led to a growing dependence on Alan for reassurance that he loved her. Having to rely on someone else to make you feel better further decreases your self-worth and can often promote feelings of jealousy.

The relationship path

Walking side by side as two individuals along the same path sets the scene for a successful relationship. In the diagram below, you can see the relative ups and downs that one couple's relationship had to endure.

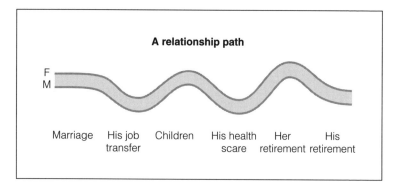

Their path altered course at different times when they were faced with different events in their lives, such as having children and changing jobs. During the different stages, one of them was more likely to be more affected than the other by what was happening. Being able to support each other is the key. It may mean that at a particular time one partner steers the direction of the relationship path more than the other. In the end, what is most important is maintaining the mindset that you are both on the path together, no matter where it leads you. Being able to negotiate the difficult patches requires commitment. Without this mindset, it's too easy to change paths.

As you will see in the next chapter, a relationship cannot succeed without commitment. Let's now look at what commitment entails.

IN BRIEF...

@ All relationships follow a path; walking side by side is what counts.
@ It is essential to maintain your individuality in your relationship.

3 Commitment

Someone asked us recently: *How do I know if we're right for each other?* The assumption behind this question is that only those who are perfectly matched will make it. The woman who asked the question was understandably puzzled. She had just learnt of two friends whose marriages had broken down. Her confusion was based on the fact that, to her, these couples seemed to have the same kinds of issues as she and her husband. She had assumed from the news that these couples had not been right for each other. She was now wondering about her own marriage.

It's easy for that question to lead to daydreams about the grass being greener in someone else's yard. Our response to the question *'Are we right for each other?'* is: *Are you committed to each other?* You see, the egg does come before the chicken in this case. If you are committed to each other and to the relationship then, providing there is no abuse occurring, in most cases you can make the relationship work. This may surprise some of you. But the fact is many people in relationships are not committed.

We wanted to address the issue of commitment early on in the book as it is the most important building block in any relationship. In this chapter we will look at the definition of commitment, the signs of not being committed, and how to make a choice about committing to a person.

What is commitment?

We like to think of commitment as being the invitation to walk along life's path together – side by side. Commitment cannot be placed on a continuum. You cannot be 'slightly committed', or 'not really committed'. It is black or white. Either you are or you're not. Remember the mindset of commitment we talked about in the first chapter? *You are the person I choose. No matter what difficulties we face, either as a couple or as individuals, I will be there for you. My behaviour will reflect the fact that I have chosen to be in a relationship with you for the rest of my life.*

Commitment means taking on the responsibility to do whatever is necessary to make the relationship work. With this definition, it is easy to see why commitment is the key to any successful relationship. It becomes the starting point. Commitment allows you to develop tolerance and acceptance. It enables you to explore some of the strategies outlined in this book in an attempt to make yourself and each other happy. If committed, you

will be more likely to be able to roll with the punches. If not, you can always be tempted to bail out.

Many people see divorce as a real option if things don't work out. By seeing divorce as an option, the incentive to really work on a relationship is reduced. Even more significantly, considering divorce as an option erodes commitment. Because divorce is more common these days, the effects of divorce on the individuals and children are underestimated. We stress that, once you are committed, the question becomes: *How can we make our relationship work?* rather than *Should we stay together?*

Some stages of the journey may be more difficult than others. Commitment keeps you on your path together. There may be times when the path follows the lead taken by only you. At other times, you will be led by your partner. You need to take responsibility for meeting your own needs within the context of walking side by side with your partner.

> *We renew our vows every time we go to a wedding – it makes us stronger; it renews our commitment to each other.*
>
> Michael, 41 years

How do you know if you're not committed?

There are clear signs of not being committed. These include: keeping the relationship a secret, flirting with someone else and threatening to end the relationship. If you do not know that your behaviour demonstrates a lack of commitment, then change is a long way off.

The reasons for not being committed are varied. You might not want to begin or maintain a relationship with someone because you do not yet believe you have the basis for a long-term relationship. That reservation makes sense, but at some stage you have to decide when to commit or, otherwise, move on. Read through our list of signs of not being committed. You may recognise some of these in yourself or your partner.

The signs of not being committed
- wanting to have a break from the relationship – *Let's have a break*
- making threats about ending the relationship
- having an affair
- communicating intimately with someone else on the Internet
- not making an effort in the relationship
- ambivalence about life goals (e.g. starting a family, financial commitment)
- keeping the relationship a secret
- pursuing someone else, even if there is no sex involved
- wanting the relationship only on certain terms
- flirting with someone else
- keeping major secrets from your partner

Joanna's story (41 years)

Steve and I were together for 13 years. We were very comfortable in each other's company right from the start. He was very easy to be around and say anything to. I guess in the early years of our relationship, I didn't analyse my needs and his actions. We just hung out together and did lots of fun things. He was a fun person. After eight years together, I definitely wanted to know whether we would be getting married or not. In retrospect, I realise our getting married was more of a progression of 'hanging out together' than making plans for the future about children, school, etc. I now realise we lacked commitment.

We also had a huge problem with my need for lots of affection and him not needing any. For some reason, I didn't realise this problem existed until after we married. Sexual problems followed, which then led to frustration, anger and resentment. After a while, I decided we couldn't live like that anymore, and I ended the marriage.

In hindsight, I know that Steve and I stayed together for too long from a young age and were probably just too afraid and insecure to split up. So we just ignored our problems.

When to make a commitment

As we have said before, there is never an absolutely perfect match for any one person. So how do you know when to make a commitment? Below is a list of factors which should help you to make the decision.

Essential factors when considering commitment

- a certain amount of passion and chemistry
- a certain amount of physical attraction
- like-mindedness
- having similar values
- bringing out the best in each other
- having spent sufficient time together in your everyday life (holiday romances are not indicative of long-term prospects)
- accepting each other's warts
- loving each other
- wanting a future together
- enjoying each other's company

If you have enough of these to go on with, make the commitment, take the risk. Once the commitment is made, you have the incentive to work on problems as they arise. You will be able to navigate through life's difficult course. You will no longer be afraid to look after your own needs and take responsibility for your own behaviour.

Premarital counselling is highly recommended at the point when you make your decision. If the decision made is an informed one, there is less chance of regret. For those of you who are contemplating or in a committed relationship, take note of our 'five Cs'. They are the five steps needed to deal with the fact that no relationship is guaranteed to succeed. They are worthwhile memorising. We often ask our couples to complete the following exercise on 'When to commit' as individuals.

The five Cs - all relationships are a risk

There is no guarantee in any relationship. The following five steps are worth remembering:

1. Choose well.
2. Commit to each other.
3. Challenge your unhelpful thinking and behaviour.
4. Confront issues as they arise.
5. Cross your fingers.

We will be examining these themes throughout the book.

When to commit

Complete the following exercise. Colour in each line to indicate how strongly you believe each of the following factors are present in your relationship. (0% = do not believe, 100% = believe completely)

	0%	25%	50%	75%	100%
Chemistry					
Physical attraction					
Like-mindedness					
Similar values					
Bringing out the best in each other					
Time together in everyday life					
Accepting each other's warts					
Loving each other					
Wanting a future together					
Enjoying each other's company					

You really need enough of each component to make a commitment. Look at the unshaded areas in your graph: as a starting point, focus your attention on these. You can then look at each component individually. For the ones that fall short of the 75% mark, you should address the reasons behind your rating.

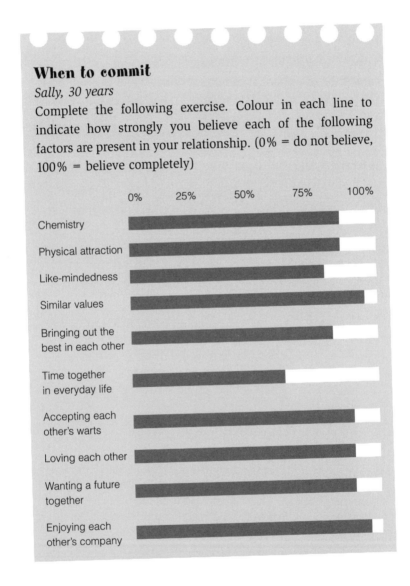

When to commit

Sally, 30 years
Complete the following exercise. Colour in each line to indicate how strongly you believe each of the following factors are present in your relationship. (0% = do not believe, 100% = believe completely)

Looking at Sally's example may help. She was in a relationship with Michael and was seriously considering marriage.

In Sally's example you should be able to see that she experienced wonderful chemistry with, and physical attraction for, Michael. She believed they had similar values and were like-minded. She certainly wanted a future with him and she said she was in love. So far, so good. The problem is her answers show that she and Michael might still be in the bubble of new love and have therefore not yet tested their relationship in everyday life. This may be blinding her to his warts; she might not have accepted them yet. We will be expanding on this notion of the bubble of new love in the next chapter. While we would say that Sally appears to have all the essential ingredients for continuing a relationship with Michael, she might not be in a position to commit yet. They would be better off spending some more time together first. It is important that Michael complete the same exercise to ensure there are no major discrepancies.

Prenuptial agreements

Prenuptial agreements, while considered necessary for some couples in some circumstances, can undermine commitment.

The assumption behind such agreements is that leaving the relationship may be an option sometime down the track. True commitment means that leaving is *not* an option.

If you are drawing up a prenuptial agreement because you have genuine concerns about the relationship, then don't commit.

When not to make a commitment

> I really loved him, but he wanted to wrap me up in cotton wool and idolise me. I couldn't live like that. My resistance to his possessive streak caused friction and so, in the end, I made the very difficult decision to end our relationship.
>
> Carol, 29 years

> We're great friends, we have the best time. Everyone tells us we're a great couple. The problem is, I am just not physically attracted enough to her. I just don't know whether it would last.
>
> Matt, 28 years

One simple motto to follow in the beginning is, 'if in doubt, don't'. Carol listened to her doubts. She was worried about her boyfriend's possessive streak. It would probably have been much easier **in the short term** to commit to the relationship and not hurt him. In the long term, Carol's fears would probably have been realised – and then she may have been suffocated by a jealous and dependent man.

> **If you are greatly concerned by some aspect of your partner's behaviour, then reconsider making the commitment.**

We are not suggesting that if you have any doubts about your relationship, you should end it. Rather, we are saying that you should not rush into a commitment before any warning signs have been thoroughly investigated.

Bad reasons to stay

There are many bad reasons for staying in a relationship. Although they may seem obvious to some, it is amazing how many people use these reasons to keep them in an unhappy relationship. Some of them include:

How I'll look to my friends or family

We have talked to many people who remain in a bad relationship because they could not face their friends or family if the relationship ended. Some report having been warned before they married that their partner was not right for them, but they ignored it. They fear hearing 'I told you so'. Others were not warned, but are still concerned that they will look like a failure in someone else's eyes. In truth, they are probably just feeling like a failure in their own eyes.

I'll never find anyone else
There are people out there who are so scared of being on their own that they will allow themselves to become more and more unhappy, rather than face loneliness. The fear of being lonely can be paralysing and can certainly prevent them from making an informed decision which would allow them to move forward.

Better the devil you know
Unhappy people fear becoming even unhappier. If you do not realise that it is possible to be in a happy relationship with someone who works with you, rather than against you, then fear of ending up in a worse situation is pretty paralysing. To overcome your fear, it is worthwhile telling yourself that you deserve to be happy. Don't put up with any devil!

If I lose this relationship, it may be too late to start a family with someone else
The clock's ticking. You thought you would be starting a family by now, but you are very unhappy. Will having children bring happiness under these circumstances? No, and the children will be the ones who suffer the most in the long run. We recommend that your relationship be very strong before you bring children into the equation.

Premarital counselling

Ideally, we recommend premarital counselling to all couples contemplating entering a committed relationship. Such counselling does not have to be just before the wedding. Preferably, it should precede the engagement, or the decision to commit. Counselling gives couples the opportunity to examine their differences and to see if they are truly compatible.

> **Premarital counselling – don't get married without it.**

Premarital counselling can be in the form of couple counselling, or as part of a group or premarital course. Premarital counselling is usually run by health professionals or the clergy. Many couples are reluctant to attend premarital counselling because they do not want to focus on potential negatives when they are in the throes of planning such a happy event. Most couples who do attend counselling tell us that they found it to be useful and positive.

There are couples who do break up as a result of counselling. This is not a bad outcome. If premarital counselling reveals problems large enough to split the relationship, then the relationship was never going to last. In most cases, couples do not break up. Rather, they discuss issues such as attitudes to money, children, household chores, spirituality and fidelity. They look at how their

> *We attended a premarital weekend which encouraged us to talk about issues at length. The whole process helped us build a good foundation for our marriage. I'm really glad we did it.*
>
> Olivia, 33 years

> *He was very keen to have some premarital counselling, but I wasn't so sure. I knew that we had some differences, but nothing that we couldn't sort out. We did go, and what I found most useful, was that we learnt **how** to sort out our differences, not just discuss what they may be.*
>
> Susan, 44 years

> *I was terribly apprehensive at first. I wondered what a priest could tell us about marriage. But I did learn a lot. Most importantly, we discovered that I had planned on keeping our money separate, while Tony had assumed we would immediately open a joint bank account. This discovery led to some heavy discussions. I'm glad we talked about it then, rather than on our honeymoon.*
>
> Michelle, 29 years

personalities and expectations of marriage differ. Communication strategies and conflict resolution skills are also taught during premarital counselling. It is far better to learn such skills when you are in your happiest state, than wait until you are struggling with certain issues.

Finally, premarital counselling can help couples to make an informed decision about their commitment to one another. And as we said at the start of this chapter, commitment comes before anything else.

IN BRIEF...

@ Commitment is a mindset. Your behaviour should reflect this mindset.

@ There is no perfect match for anyone.

@ Don't commit to anyone who is displaying behaviour that worries or disturbs you.

@ Premarital counselling helps you to make a more informed decision about commitment; helps to highlight potential trouble spots; and provides strategies for dealing with these trouble spots.

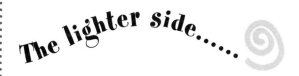

The lighter side......

What first attracted you to your partner?

He was so easy to talk to. Once we started, we talked about anything and everything. It's still the same.

Karen, 37 years

I can remember what she wore the first day we met. She was young and cute and fun to be around.

Stephen 39 years

If he liked me in a wetsuit, knee deep in mud whilst windsurfing in Narrabeen Lake then I thought he must have been keen. I liked that.

Vicki, 36 years

It was definitely something physical – that chemistry was there right from the start. I could hardly concentrate when he walked into the room.

Ellen, 36 years

I was scared to approach her. She seemed so confident and knew everybody. When I did ask her out, she was so delighted, which made me like her even more.

Noel, 32 years

It was her outgoing personality – she was really vivacious.

Michael, 41 years

I was sitting next to him on a plane bound for Nepal. The first thing I noticed was his big travel guide on Katmandu. I was desperate to find a place to stay as I hadn't had a chance to make accommodation plans. I really liked how he shared his book with me and that he didn't make any rude comments about me being disorganised. So I thought he must be a nice person, and he was!

Kathryn, 41 years

He was sensitive and a good listener.

Angela, 33 years

He had a fabulous body; broad shoulders, dark brown eyes and a really nice smile.

Katie, 33 years

We'd known each other for a long time before we got together. I really liked her and we just got on well. As time went by, I just wanted to be with her more and more. It felt very comfortable.

Paulo, 30 years

He first got my attention at a work dinner. He spoke quietly but in an open way about himself and I liked the look in his eyes.

Lauren, 42 years

I was attracted to my boyfriend physically at first before I even knew him – so I just dived right in and hoped he was a wonderful person. My risk paid off this time. I hadn't always been so lucky.

Alison, 22 years

4 | Expectations

When you enter a relationship with another person, you bring into that relationship your own expectations about how a relationship **should** be. You both have expectations about romance, sex, time spent with family and friends, and even where you will spend Christmas, to mention just a few. Some of you might not have given your expectations much thought, as they tend to be unconscious. Very few people are even aware of the influence their expectations have on the way they feel and how they react. More importantly, many people are unaware that their expectations are, at times, unrealistic.

We each experience life in different ways so it makes sense to expect that we all see the world differently. In this chapter, we will be exploring the importance of expectations in relationships. If your expectations are unrealistic, you are only setting yourself up to feel disappointed, angry or hurt, which undoubtedly will have a negative effect on your relationship. We will be looking at what expectations are, where they come from, and how you can bring them more in line with reality.

Many of your expectations about your partner are probably based on the early days of your relationship. These first months were no doubt wonderful, but they can lead to the development of unrealistic expectations in the long term.

The early days

Nothing can beat the total, all encompassing feeling of falling in love. In those early days of a new romance, all you can do is think about the other person – where they are, what they are doing and, most pressing of all, when you'll see them next. When two people fall in love their world totally revolves around each other. It's as if they have been captured in a bubble, floating aimlessly through space. Not only is there a physical yearning to be with that person, but an emotional one too.

Your bubble

Think back to the time when you were in your bubble of new love.

@ How did you feel?   @ What did you do?

The bubble and its components

What do you find in the bubble of new love? One common component that has been discussed for years is chemistry. It has something to do with the physical and sexual attraction between two people; a form of 'animal magnetism'. However, it's not the essence of a successful relationship, because chemistry waxes and wanes.

Another component of the bubble of new love is intensity. New relationships are definitely intense. Not only are they intense at a physical level but also at an emotional level, where there seems to be a pressure to gain as much knowledge about the other person as is humanly possible. It goes without saying that sex is tied up with both chemistry and intensity in new relationships. But obviously you can have sex without having either chemistry or intensity. And conversely, you can have chemistry and intensity without having sex.

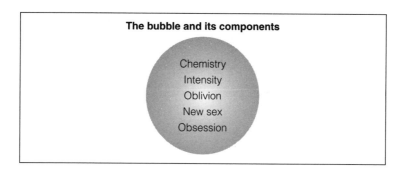

The bubble and its components

Chemistry
Intensity
Oblivion
New sex
Obsession

Why the bubble?

In the early stages of a new relationship, the role of the bubble is to protect the couple from the outside world and so enable the relationship to develop. In that sense the bubble is like an eggshell which protects a growing chick. How long it lasts will differ for every couple.

The embryonic relationship needs its bubble or shell to protect it from outside influences, such as:

@ criticism or judgement from family or friends
@ work stress
@ time pressure from family and friends
@ demands of ex-partners still in the picture
@ children from previous relationships

To allow these influences to affect the budding relationship would stifle its growth. That's why – when the bubble pops – you may find out all sorts of things about your partner and their past from which you were being protected at first.

We strongly warn couples not to make major decisions, such as marriage or parenthood, while they are still floating in their bubble. The

> *We met at a friend's wedding. I suppose looking back we were both swept up in the moment. We started going out and within seven weeks we were engaged. Within ten months of our first meeting we were married. Our marriage lasted four years. We had some pretty major differences from the outset, but they didn't get a chance to surface before our wedding. Next time I won't be rushing in so quickly.*
>
> Ian, 37 years

intensity of the bubble is not a good predictor of how long the relationship will last. Most of us have heard of people who marry very soon after meeting only to break up some years down the track.

Let's look at what happens in such relationships.

The bubble of new love encapsulates the pair. It floats along and has no anchor to the outside world. It certainly is a nice state to be in, but the old saying that 'love is blind' is true at this stage. Neither person wants to hear anything negative about either their partner or the relationship from family or friends and, in fact, the bubble acts as a filter for the real world. Kathryn and John are one good example.

Kathryn's story (32 years)

We married after a very brief courtship. I was 22 and John was 24 years old and we were so much in love. We met when we were on holidays in Fiji. Everything seemed perfect. We loved being together. John proposed after nine weeks and I immediately said yes. I couldn't bear it when my parents told me that they thought we were rushing into it. They urged me to wait and get to know him better. I didn't want anything to spoil how I felt. At the time they tried to tell me that they thought he wasn't right for me. I certainly didn't want to hear it; I could see nothing wrong. They were particularly concerned by his manner which, when I look back now, was at times very rude, and offhand to them. Over our ten years of marriage, he became that way to me and shut me out. For many years I kept my unhappiness to myself. I didn't want to hear 'we told you so', even though my parents would never have said it to me.

It's actually good when the bubble bursts

We want you to realise that when you no longer feel as though you are in the bubble phase, you have arrived at a significant moment in your relationship. The relationship has come to a crossroad, which is not a bad thing. On the contrary, if you choose to make the commitment, you can now get on with developing a mature relationship, which includes love, intimacy and hard work. As a bonus, you can also get back in contact with those people you neglected in those early stages of new love. Don't be frightened of this new stage. Don't grieve for the bubble; rather, embrace the change and rise to the challenge of taking your relationship to a higher level.

> **When you are in the throes of a new relationship, don't exclude your other friends or other activities.**

It's useful to think about how your life would be if the bubble didn't pop. Your relationship would remain mutually exclusive and, over time, the effects of this exclusion would be very damaging for both of you. You would lose your friendships through neglect. At the same time you would develop an unhealthy dependency on each other. This, in turn, would erode your confidence in your ability to make your own decisions and cope with whatever challenges were thrown your way. Maintaining a job would be extremely difficult due to those constant thoughts about each other and the desire to be together.

> **The bubble of new love has a purpose, but it's good when it pops.**

What would happen if the bubble didn't pop?

- Friends would give up on you.
- It would be hard to keep a job through a lack of concentration.
- You would not be able to test-drive the relationship in the real world.
- You would get a rude shock if children entered your relationship.
- You would not be able to cope without your partner.

But not too early...

Crises can make the bubble pop early. These include an unplanned pregnancy, sickness, death of a loved one, or work crises. These events can place a great strain on the developing relationship.

> *We had been going out for a few months when I found out I was pregnant. It wasn't planned and we both felt it was too soon to become parents. We decided that given the circumstances a termination was the only option. I found it all a bit too much. The relationship has never been the same since. We're still trying, but for how long I'm not sure.*
>
> Helen, 29 years

Because of this pressure, the relationship is forced to change gear from care-free to serious, which often leads to the premature bursting of the bubble. Many relationships break up at this point because, without the protection of the bubble, the foundation of the relationship has not yet fully developed.

The myth of the perfect relationship

Do you know of a couple who appears to have the perfect relationship? Do you think your relationship is perfect? The more perfect you believe your relationship is, the more devastated you are when something goes wrong. Further, by assuming that the relationship is perfect, you can easily fail to put in the necessary work to keep on your relationship path. Melissa thought she and David had a good relationship and was shattered to learn that David could give up on it so easily.

Melissa and David's story

Melissa told of nine years of bliss. She believed that she and David were on the same path, sharing similar goals, interests and values. Any outsider, she said, would have thought that they were the perfect couple. After a particularly bad winter of illness, when their two children seemed to be always sick and at the doctor, David began to voice concerns about his level of contentment. Melissa dismissed his comments thinking he was just sick and tired of all the illness, as she was. She didn't really notice his gradual withdrawal, being understandably preoccupied with looking after the children. He took her lack of notice as a lack of interest and withdrew further. His announcement that he was leaving shocked Melissa and all those who knew them. David did not understand why Melissa had not seen the break-up coming for months.

Although we would definitely say that it was David's responsibility to discuss his unhappiness further, Melissa's assumption that they were the perfect couple blinded her to some early warning signs.

The reality is that no matter how good a relationship looks from the outside, no-one knows what it is like to be in that relationship except the people themselves. Even then, they only see the relationship from one side. The perfect relationship does not exist. It is an absolute impossibility because individuals themselves are not perfect. If you think your relationship is perfect, or that your partner is perfect, then you are like a time bomb waiting to go off.

> *I know that perfect doesn't exist and there is no ten out of ten. But seven out of ten would be good!*
>
> Joanna, 41 years

The saint and the angel

Initially the bubble may blind you into thinking your partner is a saint or an angel. But, in fact, all the bubble does is filter out the potential trouble spots. It can be a rude shock when, one day, you realise that your partner is not the saint or angel you thought they were. It might be something insignificant, but nonetheless, you might be left feeling dumbfounded. This type of awakening usually occurs very soon after the bubble pops. The effect of your unrealistic expectations then starts to kick in.

> *He wouldn't have done that if he cares as much as I thought he did.*
>
> *Maybe she doesn't love me as much anymore.*
>
> *I thought we had the perfect relationship.*

It is important to remind yourself that your partner is not perfect and, in fact, never was. You were just caught up in your bubble, protected from the reality that is everyday life.

> **The toilet seat dilemma**
> Why do men always forget to put the toilet seat down?
> Why should men remember to put the toilet seat down?
> Why don't women learn to put it up?

So, what are expectations?

Expectations concern your hopes for the future. They are related to the way in which you live and to the goals you are striving to achieve. You have expectations about yourself in all areas of your life – in your career and in your roles as a parent, friend and partner. Your expectations are a product of your experience. The family in which you grew up and the society of which you are a part both directly influence the way you think about yourself and others.

Your childhood experience of the significant relationships around you will influence your expectations about relationships. For example, a boy who has grown up with a very domineering father and a submissive mother might have different expectations about the roles of men and women in relationships from a boy who grew up with both parents being equal.

The power of the media in the development of our expectations and beliefs about our relationships cannot be underestimated. If you believe what you read or see in the movies, then you expect relationships to be easy and glamorous. As an extension of this, you expect sex to be exciting and frequent, with sexy lingerie, soft music and candle-lit rooms.

How did you imagine your relationship?

Did you expect to marry one day and live happily ever after? Did you expect to feel 'in love' with your partner at all times? Did you expect to be able to continue to do as you pleased?

Teenagers' expectations

We asked a group of teenagers about their expectations of successful relationships. We were particularly interested in how their parents' marriage had affected these expectations. Read through some of their responses and try to remember what you expected your relationship to be like when you were a teenager. How much have these expectations changed with time and experience?

It scares me that if I get married I may not be continuously happy.

Erina, 18 years

My parents are insane because of each other and it's not a path I see myself following.

Tom, 18 years

I don't want to get married as it doesn't seem worth it.

Jocelyn, 18 years

I think I kind of expect my marriage to work and couldn't imagine it not working.

Jo, 17 years

My parents were role models for me; they were both individuals and a great couple, like pillars holding up one roof but standing separately.

Alex, 17 years

In your intimate relationships you probably have expectations about what a 'successful' relationship will entail, and what a 'good' partner will be like. The fact is that, over time, a discrepancy between expectations and reality begins to emerge. How the discrepancy is managed is a major factor in how happy you are in your relationship.

The wrong path

All my friends were married and starting to have children. I knew we had a few problems but I always said I would have a baby by the time I was 30. So, we got married. Luckily, we realised it was all wrong before we started a family.

Fiona, 35 years

If you act on unrealistic expectations you can set yourself on the wrong path. A woman who has always believed she would marry or have a baby by the age of 30 might be in danger of marrying her current partner just because she has turned 30. This is not a good basis for marriage. The influence of these types of expectations can be subtle, and can set you on the wrong path without you even knowing it.

> Unrealistic expectations of marriage set you on the wrong path.

Similarly, your expectations are influenced by your experiences in your previous relationships. For example, if your previous partner was unfaithful, you might be very suspicious or jealous about your current partner. The danger is that if these expectations go unnoticed, they can never be challenged and so their influence can be very damaging.

Children change the course

As we've said, relationships follow a path and, as the path is uncovered, so are different expectations. When a relationship is new, the expectations you have for each other, and for your relationship, will be clouded by the excitement of the moment. What happens, though, is that as you pass through different phases, your expectations are challenged and different ones are brought to the fore.

At twenty years of age, your plans for the future will no doubt be very different to your experience of life in your late thirties. It's very hard at twenty to even imagine what your life with children will be like. Therefore, the path you start on without children may not work very well when you are older. Having children certainly creates friction for many couples. The friction can be a result of competing values and desires. It can also be a product of the discrepancy between

> At university I studied to be an engineer. I couldn't wait to begin work. Moving every few months after each project finished was fabulous, until I met my wife. Then I realised that a settled family life and work on construction sites were mutually exclusive.
>
> Mike, 39 years

your expectations of each other and what actually happens in real life. Being **unaware** of the way in which your expectations influence your behaviour is the problem. Not being able to discuss these expectations and assumptions with your partner is another problem. Therefore, identifying your expectations and discussing them with your partner are the first steps.

> I had always assumed that I would have my children christened. When the issue arose, my wife was against the idea. We had never really discussed it before.
>
> Sam, 33 years

> Before we had kids we shared the chores, but now it seems as if I'm doing all of it.
>
> Janice, 33 years

I came from the US on a working holiday. We met and fell in love. I ended up extending my visa and applying for residency. Initially I was very happy, but once we had kids I became more and more unsettled. Even though I like it here, before we had children we never really discussed how we would manage this situation. Now we discuss it from time to time, spend lots of money on travel, and put the issue in the 'too hard basket'.

Louise, 35 years

We are married with two young children and I have chosen to stay at home while they are young. I would say that on the whole, we are very happy. I adore my husband and I think he adores me. But what really gets me is that he expects to play cricket on weekends as he did in the past, and I'll be there to mind the children.

Diane, 34 years

Be a team

We strongly advocate that couples with children adopt a team approach. As a starting point, it would be useful for couples to discuss their expectations of parenthood before they have children. If couples could be encouraged to understand each other's viewpoint, then they could attempt to make plans about who will and who won't do what. These plans would need to be reviewed regularly, so that both parents' needs are being addressed, enabling the couple to work together as a team. Happy parents mean happy children. Unfortunately we see too much of the 'you versus me' approach, which undermines even the best relationship.

If you are considering starting a family, then this is a great time to discuss your own expectations about how your relationship will work with children. This will help to improve your understanding of each other's behaviour. It can be the first step towards making changes so that you both feel that you are equal in your chosen roles in life. Similarly, discussions about expectations can help prevent feelings of resentment that can gradually erode the foundations of a relationship. Even if your children are teenagers, it's never too late to speak up about feelings of resentment and the help you would like.

The gap between expectations and reality

Regardless of the types of expectations you have about your relationship, the discrepancy between expectation and reality is what counts. It's easy to become dissatisfied if what you expect is dramatically different from what happens in reality. Before long a vicious cycle of dissatisfaction is established. The following diagram shows how the cycle develops. The trigger to the cycle may be an argument, a thought about something that has or has not happened, or an image. Whatever the case, the trigger to the cycle is set in motion.

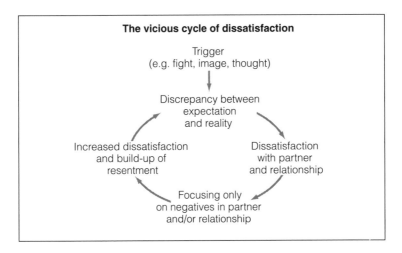

As you can see, a discrepancy between what is expected of someone and what actually happens occurs. If the discrepancy were verbalised, it might be something like: *I expected that you*

would do X, but in fact you did Y, which upsets me. From then on, a feeling of dissatisfaction about their partner and the relationship develops. The person then tends to focus more on the negatives in their partner and the relationship which, in turn, produces an increase in the level of dissatisfaction they were already feeling. If this vicious cycle continues for too long, resentment builds and builds, and relationship breakdown is a very likely outcome.

Let's look at an example of the vicious cycle in action.

We see many men who find it difficult to accept that it is quite normal for their sex lives to change after the birth of children. They expect that their sexual relationships will return quite quickly to their pre-baby levels. In all honesty, they had probably not given it much thought before they actually found themselves in that situation.

From the vicious cycle described above, you can quite easily see what happens. The trigger might be the man's initiation of sex being refused. If this happens over and over again, a discrepancy between what he expects and what is actually taking place becomes obvious. In time, he becomes dissatisfied with his partner and their sexual relationship. This dissatisfaction, in turn, makes him focus on other negative aspects in their relationship. The result then is increased dissatisfaction and the building of resentment. There is a good chance that his partner will pick up on his dissatisfaction; she might take this personally or be angered by his behaviour. Before long, she doesn't want to have sex with him because there *is* tension between them, and another vicious cycle is set in motion.

The importance of ensuring that your expectations are realistic cannot be overstated. Being open and up front with your partner is a step in the right direction. We'll show you how to change unhelpful thoughts in Chapter 6. Now let's look at adjusting those unrealistic expectations.

How to become more flexible

There are four strategies that can help you to reduce the discrepancy between your expectations and reality. They are:

1. adjusting your expectations
2. having empathy
3. developing backup plans
4. looking at past behaviour

1. Adjusting your expectations

Try to adopt a 'go with the flow' attitude. To do this, you need to become more flexible. If your expectations of your partner and your relationship are too firmly set, then you are going to be constantly disappointed. Flexibility is especially important when you or your partner are stressed. One of you might be having particular difficulties at work or with the children. You might be in a time of transition, because of the birth of a new baby, or a change of job. At such times, it is vital that you adjust your expectations of one another and try to be patient.

If ever he walked in with a 'bad day' face, I'd ask him what he needed and then I'd step into the breach.

Freda, 63 years

In times of stress, it is impossible to devote the amount of attention that you would like to the relationship. Of course, if the period of stress is prolonged, some decisions need to be made so that the relationship can be put back on the agenda.

2. Having empathy

Another way to adjust your expectations is to develop empathy by putting yourself in your partner's shoes for one moment before making that complaint. This is easier said than done, because it requires you to think hard about how a certain situation might be affecting your partner.

3. Developing back-up plans

If your boy/girlfriend often fails to call you to arrange a date, don't wait expectantly. Call them, or arrange to meet another friend. If your partner is always running late, build some flexibility into your plans if possible. Or, if you are counting on your partner to attend an appointment with you and they are often held up, organise for someone else to be on standby.

4. Looking at past behaviour

Finally, it is important to remember that the best predictor of future behaviour is past behaviour. It is amazing how many of us still expect our partner to be someone they are not. If they have always taken a long time to get up in the morning, they probably always will. If they (male or female!) have never been very good at reading maps, they probably won't develop the skill now. If they tend to fall asleep at dinner parties, they probably will continue to do so.

> **The best predictor of future behaviour is past behaviour.**

You can gain a lot of information about your partner from their previous relationships. Having a good understanding of their behaviour in other relationships may help you to keep your thinking realistic. If, for example, he spent a lot of time with 'the boys', that will most likely happen with you. If she tends to break relationships off after two years, or she left her husband for you, be

> *I listen very carefully now to what guys tell me about their ex's complaints because I usually find they are a problem for me also.*
>
> Joanna, 41 years

What are your unrealistic expectations?

Which aspects of your partner's behaviour have you been expecting to change?

I still can't get over the fact that she says she hates the phone, but chats for an hour every night.

Peter, 45 years

It always upsets me that I have to buy his mother's birthday present. Why, after 26 years, does it still surprise me?

Jillian, 53 years

How realistic have these expectations been?

warned. This is not to say that these things will definitely happen again, but at least you can be aware so that you can put safeguards in place.

Domestic IQ?

What is it?

@ a measure of a person's ability to contribute to the completion of household chores

Where does it come from?

@ family role modelling

@ some genetic basis

What can you do about it?

@ Have realistic expectations if your partner has a low domestic IQ. Change will be slow.

@ Take responsibility for asking for help if you have the higher domestic IQ.

@ Provide healthy role models for your children so they can increase their domestic IQ.

You've probably all heard the old saying that goes something like this: *A woman looks at a man and sees how she can change him, whereas a man looks at a woman and expects her to stay the same.* If your thinking is along these lines, we warn you to proceed at your own risk. You're heading into dangerous waters.

IN BRIEF...

@ Learn to be aware of your expectations.

@ If your expectations about your relationship or your partner are too high, you are setting yourself up for disappointment because your expectations will never be met.

@ Discuss your expectations about your relationship with your partner.

@ Be flexible.

@ The saint and the angel do not exist.

The lighter side.....

What do you remember from the early days of your relationship?

We talked a lot about everything. There seemed so much to learn about each other. I remember the pressure; there never seemed enough time to get enough of him.

Karen, 33 years

I felt something that I had never felt for anyone else. It's hard to describe in words, but I loved being with her, and I loved talking to her about all sorts of things that I would never have felt comfortable to talk about with anyone else.

James, 35 years

The first kiss was something I won't forget. There was a slow build to it and when it finally happened I didn't want the night to end.

Rosemary, 39 years

We were pretty adventurous in our sexual relationship. We never missed an opportunity.

Kimberley, 32 years

In the early days, we worked near each other. Every so often, I would come back to my car and there would be a note under the windscreen wipers. It would simply say 'I love you'.

Annie, 41 years

One day, he knocked on the window of my car. As I wound it down, he kissed me. That was about eleven years ago.

Charlotte, 31 years

How did you get here?

It's just too simple to say that men and women are from different planets. Each of you has been influenced by your own background. A combination of genetics, environment and experience shapes you into who you are. To understand yourself, or another person for that matter – you need to examine your past. Nowhere is your background more influential than in your relationships. Young children and adolescents learn mostly through example. The way you were taught to resolve differences, for instance, will always affect you. Therefore, the best starting point for understanding relationships is with your family history, or your 'family of origin'. In this chapter, we want to increase your awareness of the influence your background has had in shaping who you are.

Your different backgrounds

On a piece of paper, write down the answers to the following questions. Ask your partner to do the same. This exercise is intended to start you thinking about any differences between the two of you that might already be a source of disagreement, or might become a problem at some later stage.

Some basic questions about your background

- Where were you born?
- Where were your parents born?
- What is your religion (if any)?
- Are your religious beliefs important to you?
- Was your parents' relationship happy?
- What was your parents' financial position?
- What was the highest level of education that you reached?

Some of the potential sources of difficulties which could be highlighted in your answers to these questions include different places of birth, your parents' level of happiness, and different financial and educational backgrounds. We will now explore these issues in the following pages by looking at some examples. What you'll notice is that couples who don't acknowledge their differences from the outset can easily become unstuck.

> You don't have to be the same as your partner. You just need to be aware of the differences and their effects.

Different places of birth

We are seeing more and more people whose relationships are tested because they have different nationalities. This is only going to become more common as technology makes the world seem smaller. If you were born in very different places, or your parents' place of birth differs greatly from your partner's, be wary! This is not to say, of course, that we would recommend that you only match up with people born in the same place. How boring life would be! Rather, we are examining *potential* triggers of difficulties later on. Let's look at Anita's story as an illustration.

Anita's story (40 years)

I met Ted while we were both working in London. We moved in together. We shared everything. We always talked about being together for the rest of our lives. A year later we got engaged. Our families were delighted – at first. Ted is English and had always loved everything about his home and country, and was very close to his family. I am Australian and, although I loved London, I'd always planned to go home. It may seem surprising, but the subject of where we would live was never really discussed until we became engaged.

It was hard for Ted, because his family were so unhappy, but he agreed to move to Australia. He told all his mates he was moving to the end of the earth for me, which sounded very romantic at the time. We were really happy here until our son was born. Ted became horribly homesick. We took the baby over to meet all his family and friends and had a ball. It was only when we arrived home that I felt a bit worried. There was talk of another trip in eighteen months' time. I didn't know how we were going to afford it, especially as I was pregnant with our second child. He will need to get used to the idea of living here, because I am certainly not moving to the UK.

Anita and Ted's story is fairly common. It can take years before the pressure to live in the other person's 'home' becomes an issue. It might not be different countries that are the problem. Rather, one person may be from the city and the other from the country. Perhaps two people are from different states in the same country, or simply from different parts of town. The fact is that, when you are caught up in the bubble of the initial stages of a love affair, you often ignore differences in your backgrounds. In the beginning, these differences are usually highly attractive because of the novelty factor; however, they might be a source of difficulty later.

You will see this theme occurring again and again in this chapter. For Anita and Ted the problem was not that they were born on opposite sides of the world (and there are many of you in this category who do not find this issue to be a problem). The problem was that Anita and Ted did not address the issue at all. There was no insight, no flexibility – only fears and resentment.

Different cultural backgrounds

An added complication occurs when you and your partner have vastly different cultural backgrounds. Once again, if your expectations are that these differences will not affect your relationship, you will probably run into difficulties at some stage. Cross-cultural relationships are on the increase and, although this is nice to see, the potential problems have to be managed. Such problems include the influence of the extended family, the pressure to conform to traditional roles, and your own expectations of how you imagined your relationship would exist within today's society.

To tackle some of these issues, we encourage couples to discuss their expectations up front, regularly revisit the topic along the way, and try to find other people who are successfully managing

I am from an Italian background and my husband is Australian. After eight years of marriage we sought counselling when I became uncomfortable with the amount of work I was doing in the house compared to him. He expected me to take up the traditional female role, whereas I had hoped for a more even distribution of the work. In counselling, he admitted that he thought that I would have wanted things that way.

Sophia, 47 years

a similar situation. If you are contemplating a commitment to someone from a different culture, once again, we would recommend premarital counselling with someone who has an understanding of the particular issues involved.

> *I was born here, but my parents were originally from the Middle East. I never thought much about my cultural heritage until I had children of my own. I want my children to know and understand their roots.*
>
> Gus, 36 years

Different religions

Similarly, the same issues tend to arise with differences in religion. If such differences are not discussed early on in a relationship, they can easily develop into major problems, particularly when children are born. Again, we are not saying you should avoid entering a relationship with someone who is of another faith. You just need to sit down and work out how you'll manage the situations as they arise.

> *He's a Catholic, and my background is Protestant even though I don't attend any church. He is very keen for the children to be raised as Catholics. That's fine by me, as long as he takes responsibility for their spiritual education.*
>
> Jane, 37 years

> *I agreed before we had children that they would be raised as Catholics because their mother felt very strongly about it. I didn't realise that my not attending mass would be such a problem. We seem to be constantly arguing about this same issue.*
>
> Len, 44 years

> *I love him, we seem so right for each other in every way, except for one thing – his family is Middle Eastern. He says it doesn't matter, but I know it would become an issue in time. I don't think I can go through with the marriage.*
>
> Sarah, 25 years

> *I was happy to go along with some involvement in the church, but as time goes on, she seems to be spending more time at prayer groups than she does with me. I know her faith is important to her, but I think it is affecting our marriage.*
>
> Robert, 33 years

How happy were your parents?

When you were growing up, were your parents still living happily together? This is a really tricky and emotional question. It is a cliché to say that children of divorced parents will themselves divorce more easily. But why is it such a cliché? Is there an element of truth to this statement? Perhaps it would be more accurate to say that your expectations of the outcome of a long-term relationship will be influenced by the state of your parents' relationship. If all you have ever known is tension, or worse, and then separation, why would you expect things to be any better in your future? Sometimes, children living in a household full of tension will in fact go the other way, and see any disagreement as a sign of impending separation. They will therefore do anything to avoid conflict.

I remember my parents fighting at times. I also remember my mother telling me that no matter how angry or upset she was with my dad, she still loved him and they would always be together. It had a huge impact on me. I went into my marriage knowing that there would be ups and downs, but we would always stay together.

Tanya, 43 years

My parents separated before I was born. It makes me more determined to have a successful marriage and helps me to learn from their mistakes.

Carmen, 17 years

Seeing my parents happily together makes me know that I could have a good relationship.

Isabella, 18 years

If you grew up in a household in which your parents were terribly unhappy, the effect on your adult relationships can be subtle. Even without your knowledge, your family history has an effect on the way you think and behave. Being aware of the pattern of communication between your parents can at least highlight possible areas where you could focus your attention. In this way, you might stop yourself falling into the same bad habits.

> *My parents divorced when I was twelve. My dad had a drinking problem and was often verbally abusive. I ended up staying away from the house a lot of the time. I was so relieved when they split up. I do know, though, that in my own marriage I have to work very hard at tackling our problems head-on. Otherwise, it would be very easy for me to run away from them.*
>
> Tim, 39 years

Money and education matter too

Similarly, the financial and educational background of you and your parents can have an effect on your relationship. Put simply, someone from a family without much money might have a completely different attitude to spending and saving compared to someone whose family was reasonably well off. Alternatively, two people from similar economic backgrounds might have different attitudes towards money.

Again, it is not the different backgrounds in themselves that *cause* problems. Rather, it is the difference in expectations. If you are currently considering getting married or making some sort of commitment, you definitely need to discuss money and education because they are the source of many problems in relationships.

> *My husband's family didn't have much money. He's very cautious with spending and is reluctant to buy nice things for our home. We are financially comfortable and his 'saving for a rainy day' attitude annoys me at times, especially when we're talking about small sums of money.*
>
> Diana, 41 years

> *If anything, her family was better off than mine, but you wouldn't know it. They are so tight with money, and so is she. We have constant fights about saving, because I want to enjoy life while we're young.*
>
> Mike, 27 years

Couples need to have a similar 'mindset' about money. Don't get into the debate about 'my money' versus 'yours'.

One of the most common and destructive sources of conflict in relationships is not having a similar 'mindset' about money. Before making a commitment to somebody, you need to discuss how money will be handled within the relationship. We're amazed at how many couples argue over who bought the orange juice or cereal, or who pays most of the bills. A similar mindset means that you have a pool of money. This money could be kept in joint or separate bank accounts, but you should agree, as a couple, on its use. Flexibility is needed when circumstances change. Starting a family or changing jobs requires a revised plan. Without such flexibility, resentment, guilt and humiliation can creep into the relationship.

Where are you heading?

It might be helpful if you and your partner each answer the following questions.

- How would you like to be living in five years' time?
- What things would be important to you then?
- How do you measure success?

The difference between your answers and your partner's answers to these questions might be very significant. If you both have different ideas of what success means for you, you might need to make some adjustment to your goals so that they align with one another.

The influence of your personality

It goes without saying that your personality will be affected by your parents, and theirs before them. How often does your partner remind you in some way of their mother or father? How often have you actually commented on the fact? Personalities have a huge effect on relationships. Have a go at answering the following questions about your personality. Ask your partner to do the same.

How do you behave?

Please read the following statements and rate how much each one relates to your personality.

	Not at all like me				Very much like me	
I explode when angry.	0	1	2	3	4	5
I withdraw when angry.	0	1	2	3	4	5
I confront issues as they arise.	0	1	2	3	4	5
I listen well.	0	1	2	3	4	5
I talk openly and honestly.	0	1	2	3	4	5
I am an affectionate person.	0	1	2	3	4	5
I am a jealous person.	0	1	2	3	4	5
I like to be in control all the time.	0	1	2	3	4	5
I tend to choose people who have a history of violence.	0	1	2	3	4	5
I find it very easy to save money.	0	1	2	3	4	5
I find it very easy to stick to a budget.	0	1	2	3	4	5
I gamble to excess.	0	1	2	3	4	5
I tend to drink/take drugs to excess.	0	1	2	3	4	5
I am a very social person.	0	1	2	3	4	5
I would rather have a quiet night at home.	0	1	2	3	4	5
I put off doing things.	0	1	2	3	4	5
I am a very relaxed person.	0	1	2	3	4	5

The actual scores you circle in this questionnaire are not the only point of interest. What is particularly important are the differences between your scores and your partner's. A difference of one, or perhaps two, points is not significant. But a difference of three or more may highlight a potential problem. For example, if one person likes to be in control all the time, and the other generally doesn't like to be in control, sparks are likely to fly whenever the more passive partner vocalises a strong opinion on how something should be done.

But it doesn't mean that two people who behave differently shouldn't be together. On the contrary, opposites often attract, and different personalities can balance each other. However, if you and your partner have very different personalities, you do need to talk about your differences at a time when you are not upset about something, and resolve issues by working out strategies that take into consideration your different ways of behaving. We will talk more about acceptance and tolerance of each other's traits in Chapter 7. For now, we are just focusing on your awareness of the differences.

The family tree

Drawing a family tree can help you examine the influence both your parents' personalities has had on your relationship. Below is an exercise for the two of you to complete. You might not be able to complete your own family tree, but it's worth having a go.

The first step is to think about the personality style of each of your parents. List a few words that best describe how they tend/tended to be most of the time. Then select the one or two that you think fits them best. Common examples include moody, happy, cheery, aggressive, submissive and authoritarian.

The second step is to do the same for the type of relationship you believe they have/had together. Examples include: happy, volatile, resigned, average, and so on. Looking at Maddie and Greg's example (on the next page) may help you.

An interesting discussion followed from Greg and Maddie's tree. They had been living together for eighteen months when they

Your family tree

What is/was the personality style of your parents and your partner's parents? How would you describe their relationships? Have a go at doing the same for your relationship.

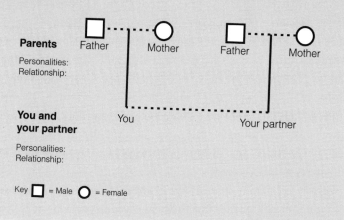

Parents
Father   Mother   Father   Mother
Personalities:
Relationship:

You and your partner
You   Your partner
Personalities:
Relationship:

Key ☐ = Male ◯ = Female

Maddie and Greg's family tree

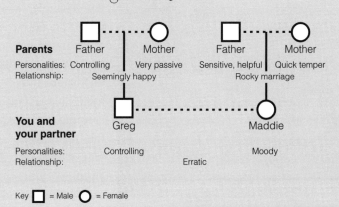

Parents
Father   Mother   Father   Mother
Personalities: Controlling   Very passive   Sensitive, helpful   Quick temper
Relationship: Seemingly happy   Rocky marriage

You and your partner
Greg   Maddie
Personalities: Controlling   Moody
Relationship: Erratic

Key ☐ = Male ◯ = Female

came to couple counselling. Greg complained that Maddie tended to alternate between losing her temper and being depressed. Maddie stated that she believed Greg was a control freak which made her furious at times and depressed at others. By looking at their family trees, they began to understand more about their personalities and that their behaviour was not just the product of *their* relationship, but of relationships before them.

Greg was very like his father, although he had never realised it before. Because his mother had been quite passive, he had **expected** Maddie to be the same to some degree. Her moods were foreign to him, and so he found it difficult to cope with them. Maddie's father, on the other hand, had been a very sensitive and helpful man. He had coped with her mother's temper by being gentle and giving. To some extent, Maddie expected Greg to do the same. This discussion helped Greg and Maddie to see that both their personalities and their expectations of each other had been influenced by their parents.

This is not to say their family histories excuse their behaviour. They are still responsible for their own actions and need to learn how to manage their feelings and behaviour.

Another important aspect of your family tree is your position in the family. Whether you are the oldest child, in the middle or the

youngest is relevant. For example, if you were the eldest and only daughter, you may have learnt a nurturing role very early and could be carrying that role into the relationship. Or, you could be the youngest and only son with five older sisters who protected you from everything.

Such a position in your family could make you expect your partner to take up the role of your older sisters.

Values and beliefs

The rules and values we were taught by our families and society at large will affect our relationship with another person. The next set of questions looks at some of these effects. There are, of course, many other effects.

Values and beliefs

Please read the following list of statements and rate how much you agree or disagree with each of them. Then ask your partner to do the same.

	Strongly disagree					Strongly agree
There was a lot of affection shown in my family.	0	1	2	3	4	5
Sexual issues were openly discussed in my family.	0	1	2	3	4	5
There was a high level of violence in my family.	0	1	2	3	4	5
Having a lot of money is important to me.	0	1	2	3	4	5
Couples should have a similar mindset about money.	0	1	2	3	4	5
Couples should share the household chores evenly.	0	1	2	3	4	5
The woman should be the primary carer of the children.	0	1	2	3	4	5
The man should be very involved in child-raising.	0	1	2	3	4	5
Mothers should not work outside the home at all.	0	1	2	3	4	5

Once again, the actual scores on these questions are irrelevant. It is the differences between the scores that are of interest. Once you are aware of the differences, you should fully discuss the reasons behind the differences. You will find that, again, your family background is a strong influence on your answers.

Let's look at Linda and Ron.

Linda and Ron's values and beliefs

Please read the following list of statements and rate how much you agree or disagree with each of them. Then ask your partner to do the same.

	Strongly disagree					Strongly agree
There was a lot of affection shown in my family.	0	1	2	3	[4]	5
Sexual issues were openly discussed in my family.	0	1	2	[3]	4	5
There was a high level of violence in my family.	[0]	1	2	3	4	5
Having a lot of money is important to me.	0	1	(2)	3	4	5
Couples should have a similar mindset about money.	0	1	2	3	[4]	5
Couples should share the household chores evenly.	0	1	[2]	3	4	(5)
The woman should be the primary carer of the children.	0	1	2	(3)	[4]	5
The man should be very involved in child-raising.	0	1	[2]	3	4	(5)
Mothers should not work outside the home at all.	0	(1)	2	3	4	5

Ron's scores = ☐
Linda's scores = ○

Linda's story (34 years)

We came from similar backgrounds in that our parents are still together, there was a lot of affection shown, there was no history of violence in either family, and our parents had the same mindset about money. We were boringly the same in terms of levels of education, and ideas on religion and money. Where we differed was that Ron's parents did not share the household chores 50:50, whereas mine did. And second, Ron's father was not very involved in his upbringing, whereas my dad was.

These differences had been briefly discussed from time to time, but did not really come up until we had children. Because of my background, I had **expected** Ron to be very hands-on with the children and help with the housework even though I was not working outside the home. Because of his upbringing, Ron loved being with his children, but he did not even think about how he could be helping me around the house.

Once we realised what was happening and why, we slowly addressed the problem. He's certainly not my dad (around the house), but neither am I his mum (in many ways).

It's not surprising that Ron and Linda's differences didn't exert their influence until they had children. This is very often the case. So, if you have not yet had children, you and your partner need to go through each statement and find out what each other thinks.

Whatever your potential sources of conflict, don't be put off. Most problems can be overcome if you have made the commitment to each other and are walking side by side through life. In the next chapter we'll start exploring ways of dealing with the conflicts that are sure to arise, beginning with the very useful skill of clear thinking.

IN BRIEF...

@ You and your partner are both products of your backgrounds.

@ You might not realise the effects your different backgrounds are having on your relationship.

@ You don't need to be with someone who is very like you. Just be aware of the differences and discuss them before you commit to a future together.

The lighter side......

Here's a little gem from the Internet (source unknown).

How to shower like a woman:

1. Take off clothing and place it in separate laundry baskets according to lights and darks.
2. Walk to bathroom wearing long dressing gown. If you see your husband along the way, cover up any exposed flesh and rush to the bathroom.
3. Look at your womanly physique in the mirror and stick out your gut so that you can complain and whine even more about how you're getting fat.
4. Get in the shower. Look for facecloth, armcloth, legcloth, long loofah, wide loofah and pumice stone.
5. Wash your hair once with shampoo with 83 added vitamins.
6. Wash your hair again with shampoo with 83 added vitamins.
7. Condition your hair with conditioner enhanced with natural crocus oil. Leave on hair for fifteen minutes.
8. Wash your face with crushed apricot facial scrub for ten minutes until red raw.
9. Wash entire rest of body with body wash.
10. Rinse conditioner off hair (this takes at least fifteen minutes as you must make sure that it has all come off).
11. Shave armpits and legs. Consider shaving bikini area but decide to get it waxed instead.
12. Scream loudly when your husband flushes the toilet and you lose the water pressure.
13. Turn off shower.
14. Squeegee off all wet surfaces in shower. Spray mould spots with bleach.
15. Get out of shower. Dry with towel the size of a small African country. Wrap hair in super absorbent second towel.

16. Check entire body for the remotest sign of a blemish. Attack if found.
17. Return to bedroom wearing long dressing gown and towel on head.
18. If you see your husband along the way, cover up any exposed areas and then rush to bedroom to spend an hour and a half getting dressed.

How to shower like a man:

1. Take off clothes while sitting on the edge of the bed and leave them in a pile.
2. Walk naked to the bathroom. If you see your wife along the way, shake willy at her making the 'woo' sound.
3. Look at your manly physique in the mirror and suck in your gut to see if you have pecs (no). Admire the size of your willy in the mirror, scratch your 'privates' and smell your fingers for one last whiff.
4. Get in the shower.
5. Don't bother to look for a washcloth (you don't use one).
6. Wash your face.
7. Wash your armpits.
8. Crack up at how loud your fart sounds in the shower.
9. Wash your privates and surrounding area.
10. Wash your bum, leaving hair on the soap.
11. Shampoo your hair (do not use conditioner).
12. Make a shampoo Mohawk.
13. Pull back shower curtain and look at yourself in the mirror.
14. Piss (in the shower).
15. Rinse off and get out of the shower. Fail to notice water on the floor because you left the curtain hanging out of the tub the whole time.
16. Partially dry off.
17. Look at yourself in the mirror, flex muscles. Admire willy size again.
18. Leave shower curtain open and wet bath mat on the floor.
19. Leave bathroom fan and light on.
20. Return to the bedroom with towel around your waist. If you pass your wife, pull off the towel, grab your willy, go 'Yeah baby' and thrust your pelvis at her.
21. Throw wet towel on the bed. Take two minutes to get dressed.

CHAPTER 6 Clear thinking

In all your interactions with other people, especially your partner, it is important that you keep your thinking on track. We now look at a really useful skill – how to think more clearly about the issues you might be facing. This skill is useful whether you are in a relationship or not. If your relationship has recently ended, it is crucial for you to understand how your thinking might be keeping you 'stuck' and preventing you from moving on. Similarly, if you are in a relationship your thinking can always be improved.

Clear thinking is based on the premise that the *way you think influences the way you feel and how you behave*. That is, it is your interpretation or opinion about a situation that causes you to feel the way you do.

Let's look at the following example: Tom, Linda and Fiona are at a dinner party. Their host tells them that a mutual friend has recently separated from his partner. This news makes Tom feel indifferent, Linda sad and Fiona anxious. The news of the separation does not in fact **cause** the feelings in each of these people, but rather triggers different thoughts which cause different feelings.

Tom is unaffected by the news because he has recently married and is very happy. Linda feels sad because the news triggers memories of her parents' bitter divorce. For Fiona, the news heightens her anxiety because it reminds her of a recent fight when her husband threatened to leave. *It's clear that the different ways these people thought about their friend's separation caused different emotions in each of them.*

Consider another example. Tracey and Scott have been going out for several months and are very much enjoying the intensity of their new relationship. But Tracey occasionally feels a little tinge of jealousy when she hears about Scott's ex-girlfriend. One night at a party, Tracey sees Scott, who is a short distance away, walk towards an attractive girl and give her a hug and a kiss. Tracey immediately feels awkward and a little jealous. She tries to fight these feelings and considers going to the bathroom. She wonders whether this woman is Scott's ex-girlfriend. Before she can leave, Scott introduces this woman to Tracey as his cousin. What happens to Tracey's jealousy? It disappears and Tracey almost instantly feels excited about meeting someone in Scott's family.

> **Changing the way you think can change the way you feel and behave.**

Automatic thinking

You are not always aware of your exact thoughts because often your thinking is automatic. For example, when performing a routine task such as driving, you are mostly unaware of the thoughts which lead to you signalling or changing gear. So in order to change your feelings and behaviour, you first of all need to identify your thoughts.

If you feel unwell or experience pain, you will probably search for the causes in an attempt to feel better. For example, imagine you are walking somewhere and you suddenly get a sharp pain under your foot. What do you do? You will probably stop and see what's causing the pain. However, if you are walking somewhere and you suddenly get a sharp pang of guilt, you will probably either worry excessively over it or try to ignore it. We encourage people to get into the habit of exploring the reasons why they feel any negative emotion. The reason will usually be some kind of negative or unhelpful thought pattern.

Inaccurate assumptions

Much of your thinking reflects the fact that you each perceive the world in a different way according to the assumptions you make. Your assumptions are usually the result of your experience. If you are looking for a new car to buy and are considering a certain make, you will automatically notice many more cars of that make on the road. As we wrote in *Motherhood,* when you are pregnant, it seems as though everybody else is pregnant too. Similarly, if your partner has recently left you, then you are more likely to notice couples in your everyday life.

> **We all make assumptions, but often these are wrong.**

But danger comes when the assumptions you make are inaccurate. If you base your judgements and ability to solve problems on inaccurate assumptions, you are heading for trouble. In order to improve the way you feel, you must identify inaccurate assumptions and then change them.

Common inaccurate assumptions about relationships

- If you feel you only *like* your partner now, that means you have fallen out of love.
  'Love' changes over the course of a relationship. It will never be the same as it was when you were in the bubble of new love.

- If you and your partner really love each other, you will spend *all* your time together.
  This assumption promotes the myth that two people should become 'as one'. It is very important to pursue individual interests to maintain a healthy sense of who you are.

- If you and your partner *really* love each other, you will *automatically* know how each other thinks and feels.
  No matter how much you love each other, it is still impossible to accurately read your partner's mind at all times.

- If you and your partner *really* love each other, you will *automatically* communicate well.
  Communication is a skill that needs to be learnt and practised.

- If you and your partner love each other, good sex comes *naturally*.
  Good sex comes from each of you having realistic expectations, being comfortable with your own sexuality, and communicating your wants and desires to your partner.

Adapted from *Living and Loving Together* by Bob Montgomery and Lynette Evans

What causes feelings?

Understanding how your thinking influences your feelings and the way you react is a vital step towards taking responsibility for making changes in your relationships. Often people mistakenly think and talk as though situations or events cause the way they feel and behave. For example:

> You **make** me so angry when you don't call.

> He **makes** me feel guilty when I don't want sex.

It is important to understand that no-one can **make** you feel angry or guilty. A situation (or action) can trigger the thoughts, assumptions, beliefs and interpretations which cause you to feel angry or guilty. In other words, it is your thinking about a situation that causes you to feel a certain way.

Therefore, you need to identify the thoughts that cause the negative emotions or feelings in the first place. Let's look at our examples:

> When you don't call, I think that you don't really want to see me and then I get angry.

> When I don't want sex, I think that I am not doing the right thing by him and then I feel guilty.

Learning to identify the thoughts that cause the feelings is central to the process of clear thinking.

How to think clearly

We can illustrate how your thoughts affect your feelings and behaviour as follows:

It seems clear that, in order to change C (your feelings and behaviour), you must change B (your thoughts), and not always look to A (the situation) as the cause of feeling bad. It is important to note that there won't always be an obvious behaviour which follows the thoughts. Sometimes it might just be 'carry on as usual'.

A ---------- **B** ~~~~~~~~~~ **C**

Situation	trigger → Thoughts	cause → Feelings/Behaviour
Neighbour does not say hello at shops.	*He must be angry with me for something I have done.*	Worried/Walk past quickly.
Neighbour does not say hello at shops.	*He really does need to get his eyes and ears tested.*	Indifferent/Go up and say hello to his face.
Husband home late. Hasn't phoned.	*Where is he? He should be here by now. He must have had an accident.*	Upset, worried/Teary.
Husband home late. Hasn't phoned.	*He's late again. Work is more important than us.*	Angry, hurt/Yell at kids.

In these examples we can see that there are at least two ways of thinking about a situation. In fact there are many more ways to think about any given situation. You will feel differently depending on how you **think** about the situation. As these examples show, the situation does not cause the way you feel, but rather triggers the thoughts that cause the way you feel.

You need to change the way you think in order to change the way you feel. You do this by challenging your thoughts once you are aware of them and then changing them into more realistic or helpful thoughts.

We want to demonstrate how negative or unhelpful thoughts can be shifted, even if only slightly. You will probably find that you are doing this some of the time anyway. The key is to become skilled at challenging your unhelpful thoughts most of the time.

Challenging unhelpful thoughts

We can expand the process in the following way:

A ----- **B** ~~~~ **C** ·········· **D** ~~~~ **E**

Situation	Thoughts	Feelings/ Behaviour	New thoughts	New feelings/ Behaviour

By challenging your thoughts (B), and turning them into new thoughts (D), the aim is to change your feelings and behaviour (C) into new feelings and behaviour (E). When people come for therapy they want to change their Cs.

It is important to note that the new thoughts (D) do not have to be falsely positive, which we would call wishful thinking. They are just realistic. The idea is not to aim for euphoria as a new feeling (E), but rather calmness, or less anger or less anxiety. This shift in emotion might then be enough to produce a more helpful and productive behaviour.

Let's look at an example. The woman has recently been left.

A ----- **B** ~~~~ **C** ·········· **D** ~~~~ **E**

Situation	Thoughts	Feelings/ Behaviour	New thoughts	New feelings/ Behaviour
My boyfriend ends relationship.	*I'll be alone for the rest of my life; I'll never have another relationship.*	Depression/ Cries, socially withdraws.	*I'm really sad that the relationship is over. I am going to have to work very hard at keeping myself busy. It doesn't mean I'll always be alone.*	Sadness/ Teary, call a friend.

Let's consider another example.

A ---- B ~~~~ C ········· D ~~~~ E

Situation	Thoughts	Feelings/ Behaviour	New thoughts	New feelings/ Behaviour
Considering marriage to a partner who has different values.	*I'll never find anyone better. I'm 33 and I want a family. He's my only option.*	Concerned, flat/Carry on as usual.	*A bad relationship is not better than no relationship. I must be true to myself. Any problems now will only get worse. I need to decide and move on.*	Happier/Seek counselling to help make informed decision.

In order to work out the new thoughts, it is often useful to ask yourself the following questions to help you find the realistic thinking that is needed to change the bad feelings or to reduce their intensity. The aim is to ensure that your new thinking is realistic, helpful and flexible.

- Where is the evidence for what I thought in B?
- What are the alternatives to what I thought in B?
- What is the likely effect on me of thinking this way?
- How would I advise a friend to think in the same situation?
- How would someone advise me?

When you begin challenging your unhelpful thoughts in this way, select simple situations, not major events. Choose an occasion when you felt a negative emotion. Perhaps you were running late for work, having a conversation or doing a household task. Remember, the situation is just the trigger, not the cause, of your negative emotion.

Challenging your thinking is a skill that should be practised regularly. We recommend that you complete the A-B-C-D-E diary

Challenge your thoughts

1. Think of a recent situation during or after which you felt angry.
2. Use the A-B-C-D-E model to identify your unhelpful thoughts, feelings and behaviour. Try to come up with the new, helpful thoughts in an attempt to change your feelings and behaviour.

A ----- **B** ~~~~ **C** ·········· **D** ~~~~ **E**

| Situation | Thoughts | Feelings/ Behaviour | New thoughts | New feelings/ Behaviour |

3. Think of a recent situation during or after which you felt upset, hurt or insecure.
4. Use the model in the same way as in step 2.

A ----- **B** ~~~~ **C** ·········· **D** ~~~~ **E**

| Situation | Thoughts | Feelings/ Behaviour | New thoughts | New feelings/ Behaviour |

format daily at first, even if it is only for one week. Initially, it's easier to practise the exercise after the event. Many people tell us that it is very hard to identify the negative thoughts, let alone challenge them, when they are feeling awful. If you are having trouble working out what you thought in a particular situation, it may help to ask:

- What did I think about myself?
- What did I think about the other people?
- What did I think about the situation itself?

By analysing the sequence of situation–thoughts–feelings/ behaviour after the heat of the moment, you can learn from your mistakes. You can then start training your mind to think more realistically and accurately. Like most things, the more you practise challenging your thoughts, the easier it will be. Once you get the hang of what you are doing, you can ease up on writing down all the examples. Then each week just select one or two examples in which your negative emotion or reaction was particularly intense. In time the challenging will become more automatic and you will notice that your thinking is more helpful, most of the time.

Being able to identify and change unhelpful thoughts provides everyone in relationships with an opportunity to do something about the way they feel. This is really good news, as being able to

think clearly and accurately is necessary for making decisions and problem solving. Remember, we are not saying that it's possible to think positively about a dreadful situation. But we are saying that it is possible to think in a more realistic way, and this will allow you to consider the options which could help the situation.

Faulty thinking

There are many types of unhealthy thinking. *Making a mountain out of a molehill* is probably well known to most of you, as is *mind-reading*. We'll now look at three other common faulty thinking errors that are problematic in relationships.

Personalising

You tend to blame yourself when things go wrong.

Faulty thinking:

> We had a fight last night. He's been so stressed at work. He came home really tired and snapped at me. I snapped back and it took off from there. I should have just let it go. It's all my fault.

Clear thinking:

> We had a fight last night. It was bad timing. He was really tired from work and obviously that contributed to how he behaved when he walked in the door. I was pretty grumpy too.

Catastrophising

You interpret events in life and death terms.

Faulty thinking:

> Our relationship is over. She's really mad at me and she won't want to go out with me anymore.

Clear thinking:

> *I need to see her soon and find out what she is thinking. I won't know until I discuss with her what happened.*

Selective thinking about the negatives

You look on the negative side, dismissing the positive aspects of your relationship.

Faulty thinking:

> *He's got yet another late meeting. I'm fed up. This relationship is going nowhere.*

Clear thinking:

> *He does work very hard but he is always home on weekends. Maybe he's not happy about his work load either.*

'What if...?' and 'Should' statements

Two other thinking traps into which people fall are 'What if...?' and 'should' statements. 'What if...?' statements are hypothetical questions based on something that has not even happened and might never happen. There is an expectation that the worst case scenario is likely and that you might not be able to deal with the event.

Go back to our clear thinking model. If your thoughts (B) include 'What if...?' questions, then you are most likely to feel anxious or scared (C).

For example, Rebecca identified the following unhelpful thoughts when she was approaching her wedding day.

> *What if he leaves me? What if we end up getting divorced?*

Her thinking needed to be challenged as Rebecca was literally making herself sick worrying about the worst case scenario. It helped Rebecca to challenge her thinking in the following way:

I have no evidence to suggest that he will leave me and we'll get a divorce. We're not even married yet. There will, of course, be some tough times and we'll both need to ensure that we tackle these head on. I'm committed to making it work.

Let's look at another example using the A-B-C-D-E diary format:

A ---- B ~~~~ C ·········· D ~~~~ E

Situation	Thoughts	Feelings/Behaviour	New thoughts	New feelings/Behaviour
Wondering about getting married and having children.	*What if he's not my perfect match?*	Uneasy, anxious, ambivalent/ Procrastinate.	*There's no perfect match or relationship. We do get on very well.*	Less anxious/Plan to discuss future with partner and make decision.

Similarly, 'should' statements reflect faulty thinking. If the words 'should', 'must' or 'ought' make up part of your thinking about yourself in (B), then you will most probably feel some degree of guilt in your feelings (C).

For example, Donna thought:

I should go sailing with him on Saturdays.

The use of the word 'should' implies that Donna would like to be doing something other than sailing with her partner on Saturdays, but she feels guilty if she doesn't go sailing with him. Her thinking needs to be challenged in the following way:

I will go sailing with him some of the time, but I have other things that I would also like to get done on weekends and that's okay.

If your 'should' statements are directed towards your partner (B), then you will most likely find that you have feelings of anger, irritation or resentment (C). For example:

She should want to go out late on Friday nights with me.

A more helpful way of thinking is:

It would be great if she wanted to stay out late on Friday nights but I know she has worked hard all week and gets tired more easily. I will either go out alone or have a quiet night with her.

By changing the language you use in your self-talk, you relax your expectations. This is particularly important for promoting an attitude of 'going with the flow' in relationships.

Use a diary

Regardless of what type of negative emotion or reaction you are experiencing, have a go at recording your thoughts, feelings and behaviour in the diary format in order to become more aware of the way you think. Use a book and set up the columns just as we have done. This allows you to keep track of your negative thoughts and their consequences. Date your entries and you'll be able to check your progress. After a while, you will probably see some common themes in your thinking emerge. This will give you an idea of where you might need to focus more of your attention. We suggest that you include examples that are related to both your relationship and incidences that concern you as an individual.

Even though it might seem really tedious to complete this exercise on a regular basis, we believe it is a valuable skill for everybody to learn. At first, keeping a diary might seem awkward. But the more effort you put into keeping the diary, the more benefit you will gain. We cannot emphasise this enough. Many people fall into the trap of just doing it in their heads. In our experience, people make more gains if they write their examples down, because more cognitive processing is required to put pen to paper. But be patient – as it might take a while to retrain your brain into thinking realistically.

Keep your own diary

For the next week, have a go at keeping a diary in the way we have outlined. There is a master sheet on page 212 for you to copy. Don't forget to include both individual and relationship examples.

IN BRIEF...

@ Thinking differently about a situation can make you feel better and behave differently.

@ Identify the assumptions you make.

@ No-one or nothing can make you feel a certain way.

@ Change your unhelpful thoughts using the clear-thinking approach.

@ Keep a diary about your thoughts, feelings and behaviour in the way we've described.

The lighter side......

Ten most common complaints about men
1. Leaving the toilet seat up

2. Revving the children up before bed
3. Wanting sex all the time

4. Not doing chores
5. Not coming home when they say they're coming home

6. Playing golf every week

7. Wanting sex all the time

8. Reading the mail as soon as they walk in the door
9. Being able to tune out from the outside world whenever they're watching TV
10. Stepping over anything left lying on the floor

Ten most common complaints about women
1. Finding it hard to sit still when people are visiting
2. Talking non-stop on the telephone
3. Re-doing what their partner has just done
4. Not wanting sex all the time
5. Tendency to listen to girlfriends' or mother's advice more than partner's

6. Seeking constant reassurance about how they look
7. Nothing ever seems good enough for them
8. Washing anything not on a body
9. Difficulty forgetting partner's past wrongs

10. Always wanting something new for the house

Warts and all

One of the hardest things we ask our couples to do is to accept each other 'warts and all'. The old saying that *you can't change your partner* is very important for two reasons. First, trying to change your partner is a futile exercise. They are who they are and you probably **used to love them for it.** Second, we would encourage you to look inwards and see what you can change in your own behaviour rather than in your partner's. In this chapter we outline some strategies to help you to accept more readily your partner's faults or their irritating ways.

You probably used to love their warts

We asked some couples what first attracted them to each other. We then asked them if there was any behaviour to which they had been attracted initially, but now found irritating. Here are some of their responses.

> *I thought she was so clever. She could talk on any subject. Now I get annoyed that she thinks she knows everything.*
>
> Brian, 42 years

She was so caring, always putting herself last. I now wish that she'd do more for herself.

Guilio, 60 years

He was ambitious and doing well even when we met. That was attractive to me. Over the past few years, I feel as though I'm very low on the list of priorities.

Catriona, 39 years

I was attracted to his sense of humour. Now I get so frustrated because he never takes anything seriously.

Patricia, 31 years

He was so laid back and relaxed. Twenty years on, I realise he's just a lazy slob.

Suzanne, 45 years

Wendy and Richard's story is a good example of the problems which can arise when you forget the person you married. They came for couple counselling and were on the verge of splitting.

The bubble blinds you to your partner's warts. They have always been there.

Wendy and Richard's story

Richard: *I was from a strict family. My mother believed that children should be seen and not heard. I couldn't wait to have my own family.*

Wendy: *My parents were very loving. I always knew I would be all right, as long as I stuck with my family. I just presumed having my own family would be the same.*

Richard: *I thought we were a perfect match. Wendy would love me and any children we would have in a very different way to my mum. We got married and had a son and a daughter. Nothing has been as I'd hoped. Wendy is so soft on the children. She doesn't push them at all and lets them get away with murder.*

Wendy: *I've got to be gentle on them. Richard is so pushy and tries to make their choices for them. It's hard on the kids, and me. We just don't see eye to eye on much at all when it comes to the children.*

When Wendy and Richard came to us for couple counselling, we asked them, before anything else, what had attracted them to each other.

Wendy: *Richard was so strong and determined. I felt secure and trusted him to look after me.*

Richard: *Like I said before, she was so loving and affectionate – the opposite of my mother.*

In a nutshell, counselling attempted to develop a team approach to their parenting, making use of both their strengths. They were also reminded of what they initially found attractive about each other. They then looked at how they could alter their thinking to be less critical and more constructive of each other's approach.

The test will be whether Richard and Wendy can change their unrealistic expectations of each other once they re-examine what attracted them to one another in the first place.

Most behaviours strengthen with age

Think back to why you were attracted to each other in the first place. Now think about some of your recent disagreements. How much have they related to basic personality differences which you had originally found attractive? Personalities do not weaken with age – quite the opposite. The 'laid back' person becomes lazier in their partner's eyes as they age. The person who showed a lot of strength and direction may be perceived by their partner in later years as a 'control freak'. With the strengthening of certain behaviours comes increasing intolerance from, and towards, your partner. This intolerance is increased because, with time, you and your partner remove your rose-coloured glasses. Now you both see things more clearly.

One of the main purposes of this chapter, and indeed the book in general, is to work out ways to be more tolerant and accepting of each other's personalities. Commitment to your partner needs to be converted into a decision to work **with** rather than against your partner's personality. It's actually fairly easy to predict how someone will react to circumstances later in life. You can simply look at the way they behaved in early adulthood. In that way, their personality is already obvious. Despite this knowledge, it's not uncommon for people to still hold onto unrealistic expectations about their partner's behaviour. In fact, expectations often become more unrealistic as time goes by. So, the next time you wish your partner would behave in a certain way, ask yourself: *How do they usually behave in similar circumstances?*

Life stress affects your relationship

> A relationship has a good chance of success if the individuals adapt well to change by developing acceptance and tolerance.

'Life events stress' is a term used to relate the impact of certain events that occur in a person's life to their health and wellbeing. Major life events include the death of a partner, marriage, unemployment, divorce, change of financial state, and having a baby. Psychologists look for how much change a person is going through in their life, in order to predict a person's future health, regardless of whether the change is considered positive or negative. Marriage, for example, is considered a positive event, but it can result in about the same amount of stress as being fired or suffering a personal illness or injury.

Even if, as an individual or as a couple, you have not had to face major issues such as the ones listed above, life itself is still stressful. The effects of having to make a living, and balancing

family and work life, are occurring *even though you might not be aware of them*. Stress exerts its effect on all areas of your life. You may be tired, irritable or tearful at times. It's important to understand that stress affects your relationship too. We can illustrate the effects using the following graphs.

In both graphs, you can see that there is a baseline level of stress. This baseline stress level represents the minimum amount of stress we experience in life. Just surviving each day, whether good or bad, creates a certain level of stress. As everyday life goes on, your stress level (shown by the wriggly line) rises and falls. Everyone has a coping threshold which is determined by a number of factors, including personality and experience. Once your stress level rises above your coping threshold, it becomes very difficult for you to feel as if you are coping. The key to being able to handle the rises and falls in life is to keep your stress level below this threshold.

In the first graph, you can see that the baseline stress level is low enough to accommodate the rises and falls of day-to-day stress. In this state, life is going on, but the low baseline means that the rises do not go above the person's coping threshold.

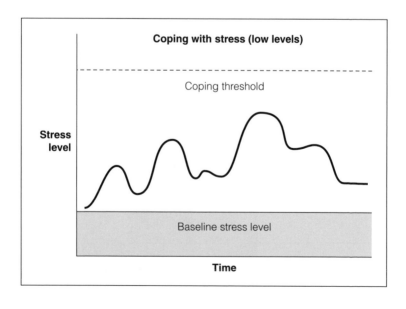

Coping with stress (low levels)

Coping threshold

Stress level

Baseline stress level

Time

The second graph illustrates what happens with time if different life events are not managed. The stress of life itself can cause the baseline stress level to rise. The individual therefore feels the effects of day-to-day life much more because the rises send the person over their coping threshold.

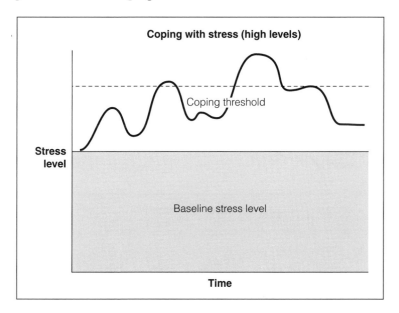

Coping with stress (high levels)

Coping threshold

Stress level

Baseline stress level

Time

You can see that the same rises and falls occur in both graphs. The difference lies in the increased baseline stress level. We often see that, in times of stress, people's relationships suffer. Problems start to occur because the individuals are unaware of the increase in the baseline stress, and blame their partner for their inability to cope with the rises and falls.

Pam came for help because she could not understand why she was so irritable with her husband and children. Part of her treatment included looking at the effects her choices had had on her. She could see that, although the choices were mostly positive, they still caused her baseline stress level to rise. Getting married to Steve and having their first child were extremely happy events for Pam, but both events had caused a rise in her baseline stress level. Returning to full-time work after having the baby sent her stress level over her coping threshold. Deciding to work part-time after the birth of her second child subsequently reduced her stress level.

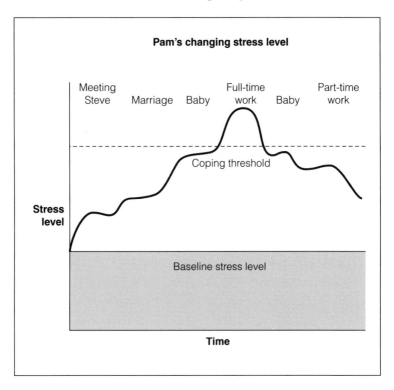

How to lower baseline stress

As we have said, everyday living produces a certain amount of stress, and some of the events we experience cause our baseline level of stress to rise. This is not the end of the story. It is possible and necessary to stop every now and then and look at ways to decrease your baseline stress level. The following list could help you to achieve this aim.

- Book a holiday.
- Book a baby-sitter and then decide what to do.
- Leave the washing or cleaning and go for a walk.
- Turn off the news and put on some relaxing music.

- Plan less to do in each day.
- Factor extra time between appointments to avoid rushing and increase flexibility.
- See a counsellor.
- Have a massage.
- Try to exercise regularly.
- Read a good novel.
- Do something creative.
- Challenge unhelpful thoughts.
- Visit or phone a friend.
- Take the occasional long bath.

You can change your perception of the warts

Not only does someone's behaviour strengthen with age, but your **perception** of their behaviour and their warts changes over time. You can see by the two graphs above that everyday events cause stress which, in turn, places strain on a relationship. The strain can take the form of using your partner as the scapegoat for the problems in your relationship.

It is fairly common practice to react to the behaviour of your partner because you're frustrated with, or intolerant of, similar behaviours in yourself. Many people tend to criticise others for the things they often do themselves. The most opinionated people, for example, are quick to judge someone else for speaking their mind. This tendency is often played out in relationships. Therefore, before criticising your partner's behaviour, first examine whether there is something you would like to change in yourself.

Focusing more on your partner's faults or warts ends up becoming a habit. The danger is that you can start to become very sensitive about a certain behaviour, rather than seeing it as part of their personality. Look at Megan and Ariane's conversation about their husbands' behaviour.

Megan and Ariane's conversation

Megan: *He's just so lazy. I put a basket right beside his side of the bed so that he wouldn't have to strain himself to put his dirty clothes in it. Even when I was really sick last week, he didn't pick up his game – he just left everything to build up until I got better.*

Ariane: *Mike's the same. No matter how many times I ask him to put his clothes in the laundry, he won't do it. I hate the sound of my own voice sometimes, so I just do it myself.*

Megan: *He really mustn't care much about me. If he did, he would help out a bit more. He certainly would be more supportive when I was sick! I get more down about it than angry.*

Ariane: *It's not because he doesn't love you. Craig is the same as Mike. They had mothers who did everything for them. We can't really expect them to change overnight the way they have always done things. I suppose we just have to keep trying and in time (with a lot of nagging) maybe they will be more helpful.*

This conversation is very interesting because the same behaviour in the men caused different reactions in the women. The different reactions were caused by the women's different perceptions or interpretations of the behaviour. If we were talking to Megan, we would use clear thinking to challenge the way she interpreted Craig's behaviour. In a way, that was what Ariane was doing. She was challenging the way Megan was thinking about the situation. More formally, we would challenge Megan's thoughts in the following way:

1. Where is the evidence that Craig not putting his dirty laundry in the basket means that he doesn't care about you?

2. What would you say to Ariane if she were complaining that Mike didn't love her because of the same behaviour?

After looking at these questions, we can set the example out in the following way:

A ----- B ~~~~ C ·········· D ~~~~ E

Situation	Thoughts	Feelings/ Behaviour	New thoughts	New feelings/ Behaviour
Craig not helping when Megan sick.	*He doesn't care about me.*	Hurt/Not talk to him.	*What should I expect? His mother always picked up his clothes. He lived with her for twenty years. We've been together only eight.*	Less hurt, calmer/Talk to him again.

You can see that in Megan's mind, Craig's behaviour was directly linked to his feelings for her. Once she was able to challenge her thoughts, she found the road a lot smoother.

Look at the different ways the following situation is perceived.

The link between perception and behaviour

Situation: Your partner seems preoccupied and disinterested in you one night.

Perception A = *She's not interested in me at all. Her job is more important to her than me.*
Perception B = *She must have something really important on her mind. I will give her some space to focus on her problem for now. If it goes on too long, I will ask her if I could help her to solve it.*

Of most interest is the behaviour that follows the different perceptions.

Behaviour A = Alternate between ignoring her and making snide remarks.
Behaviour B = Get on with own thing.

Which behaviour would be more likely to not only solve the problem, but also lead to both individuals feeling OK?

> *You don't marry someone who is perfect, you marry someone whose faults you can live with.*
>
> Donna, 40 years

So it is really important to get into the habit of interpreting your partner's behaviour as a reflection of them, not you. And remember, no-one is perfect. We all do things that irritate others.

Check that your expectations are realistic

We hope you can see that clear thinking can help you to accept your partner's warts. We are not suggesting that whatever your partner does is totally right and that you should just accept it. Rather we are saying that you need to be realistic in your expectations of your partner, given their personality and family background.

Megan's expectations of Craig, considering the way his mother had always looked after him, were unrealistic. If we were to ask

Megan about his background, she would no doubt be fully aware of all that his mother did for him. With the building of baseline stress as a result of everyday living, this aspect of his past had been forgotten, and her expectations had become unrealistic.

Jennifer was another whose expectations had become unrealistic over time. She came for counselling because she was hurt and angry that her partner's family was not very interested in their children. She had tried every way she could think of to involve them in their lives. Time after time she was hurt by their resistance. What angered her most was that her partner did not help her in this quest. The issue was putting an enormous amount of strain on their relationship. Her unhelpful thoughts were as follows:

> I find it hard to believe that these people do not care about their grandchildren. It's as if they are not good enough for them. My partner mustn't care much about me or the children either, or he would make them see more of us.

When Jennifer was asked about the history of their relationship with her in-laws, she said that they had never seen much of them. Her partner had never been close to his family when he was growing up and had moved out of home at an early age. He was happy to see them once or twice a year during the holidays. She had been happy to not see them much before she had children, but had been hoping and **expecting** things to change once they had children. What was affecting her most was her disappointment in her partner not standing up to his parents. Clear thinking once again helped to challenge the unhelpful thoughts in the following way.

A ----- B ~~~~ C ·········· D ~~~~ E

Situation	Thoughts	Feelings/Behaviour	New thoughts	New feelings/Behaviour
Partner not telling his parents to be more involved with their children.	*He doesn't love our children enough to take on his parents.*	Hurt/Constant fighting.	*What should I expect? His family hasn't changed. It doesn't mean he doesn't love his kids.*	Less hurt, calmer/Get on with our lives.

In counselling, Jennifer was able to readjust her expectations of her partner and his family so that she was able to concentrate on their lives and, eventually, the hurt lessened.

Your and your partner's warts

What, in your eyes, are your partner's warts?

What would your partner say are your warts?

'You're just like your...!'

These words are often said in the heat of the moment. It is a throwaway line which can cut very deeply. Let's think about what the words mean. They refer to the fact that your partner has some personality characteristics in common with one or both of their parents. Is that surprising? If it is, then this chapter will hopefully help you to align your expectations with reality. If it is not surprising, just irritating, then some work needs to be done on increasing your acceptance of your partner's warts. Once again, those warts have always been there. They might even have been part of what attracted you to this person in the first place. The question is, what do you do about your irritation?

Accepting that these warts have always been there, just not in such an obvious way, is a start. Second, you can look at ways to ask for help with *your* irritation about the behaviour. A good way to do this is to have a discussion based on the answers you both give to the following questions.

How are you like your parents?

@ Are you similar to either of your parents?

@ Looking at any similarities, which would you like to keep, and which would you rather weren't there?

@ What can you do about them?

As a couple, if you can sit down and answer these questions, you will probably find that your partner also has the same fear of being like one of their parents in a certain way. It is possible to work as a team and attempt to keep in check some worrying behaviours on either side. If you can discuss this strategy when neither of you is upset, it's amazing what change can be achieved.

Warning – Domestic violence is not okay

Domestic violence is a crime. It includes a range of violent and abusive behaviours perpetrated by one person against another where the couple is either married, in a de facto relationship, or is separated or divorced.

Domestic violence includes:

@ physical assault
@ sexual assault
@ emotional or verbal abuse
@ economic abuse – restricted access to money and property

What are the effects of domestic violence?

@ reduced self-esteem
@ loss of confidence
@ loss of a sense of control
@ inability to make decisions
@ social withdrawal

If you are a victim of domestic violence

@ Do not accept it.
@ Contact your local domestic violence hotline.
@ Call the police.
@ Seek individual counselling.

Note: Couple counselling is not appropriate when domestic violence is involved. Abusive behaviour is not a wart that needs to be accepted.

Pick your fights

It's very easy for the positive side of a relationship to become eroded by the problems you face and by each other's faults. This erosion just leads to further exposure of the warts and they can therefore have an even greater negative effect on the relationship. One way to minimise this erosion process is to first own the problem and then pick your fights.

By owning the problem, we mean that you need to accept the fact that you are the one who is annoyed by a certain behaviour. *Therefore it is your problem*. It cannot be up to your partner to be on the constant lookout for any of their behaviours that might annoy you. This may be hard to accept – especially if the behaviour is really selfish or inconsiderate. But because your partner's behaviour is not irritating them, there is no incentive for them to change. It is your irritation, therefore your problem.

Once you have accepted the problem as your own, you need to decide whether it is worth addressing. There are many issues in life, but time passes too quickly for us to tackle all of them. Over time, it is worthwhile concentrating on those issues most important to you (and your family). By picking your fights, you can learn to accept and ignore the more insignificant behaviours, so that when you do tackle something, it becomes clearer that the issue is really important to you. It might help to ask yourself *before* you pick a fight: *Will I be worrying about this in a year's time?* If the behaviour is extremely selfish or inconsiderate, then the answer to this question will be *yes* and therefore you will need to address it.

> **Own your problem. If an issue which irritates you does not irritate your partner, there is no incentive for them to initiate a resolution.**

The following exercise may seem unnecessary and unnatural, but the idea can really help. Most parents will tell you that they have to pick their fights with their children so that the really important behaviours are shaped. The same principle applies to your relationship with your partner. By picking your fights, you can avoid a lot of hurtful arguing that at the end of the day is pretty insignificant in the scheme of things.

> **You do have a choice as to whether or not you pick a fight.**

Hierarchy of irritating behaviours

A. Think of the five most irritating things your partner does. Rank them in order from least to most irritating.

B. Accept that it is *your* problem that they irritate you.

C. Starting with the least irritating behaviour, see how long you can ignore it. It may help to use clear thinking to challenge the thoughts that lead to your irritation.

D. If you can let go of the least irritating behaviour, start work on ignoring the next behaviour on the hierarchy.

E. When you get to the point that the behaviour can no longer be ignored, because you can't change the thoughts that are making you feel irritated, tackle the issue with your partner. If you have accepted that it is *your* problem, the discussion should not seem like an attack.

It might be useful to work out ahead of time a realistic thought that helps you rise above the irritation. Useful questions to ask yourself are:

- Does X really matter in the scheme of things?
- Are there any benefits in not tackling this issue now?
- What do I have to lose if I choose to pick a fight about X?

Here is how Jim used the hierarchy of irritating behaviours to tackle some of his problems with his partner Judy.

Jim's hierarchy of Judy's irritating behaviours

A. *The five things I find most irritating about Judy (from least to worst) are:*

    (1.) Talking every night on the phone to her friends.

    (2.) Reading in bed every night when I want to sleep.

    (3.) Calling me at work three times a day.

    (4.) Constantly reminding me to ring my parents.

    (5.) Telling me what to do with the children.

B. *I realise that these behaviours are my problem because they upset and irritate **me**.*

C. & D. *I have successfully ignored her talking on the phone most nights and reading in bed every night.*

E. *I can't just ignore her calls to me at work because they interrupt my day. I have gently suggested she write down what she wants to talk to me about when I'm at work and save it up for one phone call. I will also make a point of ringing her. I have asked her to let me take responsibility for ringing my parents. We are currently working on how she can relinquish control over the children when they are with me.*

This strategy freed Jim up so that he could tackle the most important issues and stopped him feeling as if the whole relationship was a strain. Most importantly, it allowed Jim to take responsibility for the change that took place, since these were *his* issues.

IN BRIEF...

- @ You need to accept each other – warts and all.
- @ Personalities strengthen with age.
- @ Relationship success can be related to an ability to develop acceptance and tolerance.
- @ Clear thinking reduces the effects of the warts.
- @ If there is abuse involved, it is not okay.
- @ Pick your fights.

The lighter side......

Was there anything about your partner that used to attract you, but now irritates you?

I liked the fact that he knew so much about sport. Now that seems to be all he knows.

Wendy, 37 years

*I liked the fact that he **used** to weigh more than me.*

Tahinee, 39 years

I can't think of anything that didn't always irritate me.

Linda, 37 years

I found him to be troubled, angry and brooding. That was attractive to me until I realised that I was married to a moody bastard.

Marie, 38 years

I used to like it that she was so chatty and now she never seems to shut up.

Dougal, 45 years

She was so capable. I now find her emasculating.

Jeremy, 37 years

She told this joke really well and I loved that. Twenty years later, she is still telling the same joke and it's not funny anymore.

Patrick, 39 years

I was attracted to the fact that he wasn't such a boy like other boyfriends had been. I have to laugh now that he hides from the handyman I have had to call to fix things around the place.

Elizabeth, 40 years

I loved her femininity, but I hate living in a pink-laced palace.

Andrew, 33 years

He's so relaxed that sometimes it's hard to get him moving.

Nance, 33 years

I used to like the fact that she wasn't a neatness freak like my mother. Now I just wish I could find my shoes.

Richard, 41 years

She used to look so well rested. Now I know why!

David, 38 years

8 | CHAPTER

Own your problem

We introduced the idea of owning your own problems in the previous chapter. There, we were looking at taking responsibility for **your** irritation about certain behaviours or elements of your partner's personality. Remember, we are not saying that your partner should never address their own behaviour, rather they are unlikely to initiate the change because they do not see their behaviour as a problem.

In this chapter, we want to expand on the idea of owning your problems. We want to look at how changing **your** behaviour can often improve your relationship. We also want to demonstrate how learning to become more reliant on yourself, rather than depending on your partner, is liberating and really benefits the relationship.

Whose problem is it?

Whenever anyone describes to us a difficulty they are having in their relationship, we immediately ask them: *Whose problem is it?* We do this to save time. If we don't, the person invariably goes down the path of assuming it is their partner's responsibility to make them happy. While we're sure your partner does indeed want you to be happy, it cannot be their responsibility. Just as it is not your responsibility to make them happy.

Communication skills training is often seen as the panacea for all relationship difficulties. While it is true that in many relationships communication is far from ideal, will learning to tell the other person how you are feeling or what you are thinking solve *your* problems? As we have said, gone are the days when couple counselling focused on what your partner needs to change to make you happier. We have now shifted our approach to help individuals take responsibility for their own happiness and their own problems.

We see a lot of couples who proudly announce that they know they have communication difficulties and expect that a session or two with a psychologist will set them on the path to bliss. Tony and Andrea were one such couple.

Tony and Andrea's story

Tony: *We've been together for eight years. We moved in together five years ago and had our son three years later. I just love being a dad.*

Andrea: *I love being a mum too. The first six months were great. But then I went back to work full-time. I love my job. I love our son. I'm happy with our childcare arrangements. I'm just not happy with Tony! He's just so slack. Even though we are both working full-time, I'm the one who does all the jobs at home. He doesn't even notice what needs to be done. I tell him time and time again that I'm sick of it, but it doesn't make any difference.*

Tony: *I am so sick of the nagging. I mean, what's more important, playing with Saxon, or vacuuming the house? I wonder why she bothered to have a child if all she cares about is the state of the house.*

Tony and Andrea's issue is a very common one for couples with young children. The most significant statements made in Tony and

Andrea's story were made by Andrea. First, she stated that: *I'm just not happy with Tony!* Second, she said: *He doesn't even notice what needs to be done.* The significance of these statements should become more obvious as you read this chapter. For now, we can tell you that it is **Andrea who has the problem. She** is not happy with Tony. *He* isn't even aware that a problem exists.

Although Andrea had hoped that counselling would show Tony that he needed to be more helpful, the result was quite different. As usual, we asked the couple: *Whose problem is it?* To encourage Andrea to own the problem, we asked her the following questions:

1. Who is aware of the problem?
2. Who is suffering as a result of the problem?
3. Whose responsibility is it to address the problem?

Andrea's answers to these questions were as follows:

1. *I am. He doesn't even know why I'm always so upset.*
2. *I am. He just gets upset at me nagging.*
3. *Mine; if it's not an issue for him, why would he just do what I want?*

We are not saying that Tony should never help with the housework. What is important here is that the responsibility of the problem is given to the right person. Andrea was right. If an untidy house is not an issue for Tony, then it will not be on his mind and he won't notice it. Therefore, where is the incentive for Tony to change? Once Andrea owned the problem, we were then able to address how she was going to resolve it. Exactly how this was done is outlined in the following chapter.

Mind-reading and false expectations

The biggest problem with not owning your problem is that you expect your partner to read your mind and know what will make you happy. This expectation is unrealistic and you will be constantly disappointed and resentful. Life would be very tedious if you had to anticipate what others wanted. It would be like treading on eggshells, worrying about upsetting everyone. It is far simpler, and healthier, to walk around assuming you have done nothing wrong until someone tells you otherwise.

Further, not having to rely on someone else to read your mind and be responsible for your happiness is liberating. Just think about it: you are upset about something. You have to wait until, first, your partner notices that you are upset and then rely on them being able to read your mind and know what you want them to do about it. You will probably spend your life waiting – and it will not be a happy wait. Or, once you know you are upset about

> When you attempt to read your partner's mind, you are likely to be incorrect.

something, you take responsibility for the problem and set about looking at how to resolve the problem. Owning the problem in this way leads to a much healthier sense of control. You become responsible for having your needs met, making specific requests and for expressing your hurts and disappointments.

The selfish–selfless continuum

Concentrating on having your own needs met might sound selfish to some. It depends on your definition of selfishness. We define 'selfishness' as putting yourself first to someone else's detriment. Obviously, in relationships, there will be people who do fit into this category. When you are in a relationship, it can also be easy to slip into a habit of being selfless. We define 'selflessness', as putting another first to your own detriment. When someone suggests to the selfless, passive person that they think more about themselves before it is too late, they often worry about becoming selfish.

The problem with this line of thinking is that it is too black or white. You are neither selfless nor selfish. There is a grey area. We can put the black, the white and the grey on a continuum in the following way:

Selfish	**Self**	**Selfless**
Putting yourself first to the detriment of your partner	Considering yourself as well as them	Putting your partner first to your detriment

On this continuum you can see that, in order to be considered selfish, your partner has to suffer for you to gain. Therefore, if you are considering your needs and your partner is not actually suffering, you are merely considering yourself; you are not being selfish. It is desirable to be as close to the centre of this continuum as possible: not too selfish, but not too selfless. Placing yourself in the centre of this continuum helps to develop a healthy you, and reduces the need to rely on someone else to tell you that you are worthwhile. In the end, your relationship will benefit.

What are my needs?

If you are already in the habit of relying on assurance from your partner and behaving in a selfless way, you might not know what your needs actually are. The following exercise could help you to work out what they might be.

It's true that you would not always be aiming to do what you want to do, but it does become a concern when one partner is rarely

About me

For each of the following areas, list what you would like, what your partner would like for you, and what actually ends up happening. Here's one done by Marilyn, 44.

Areas	What I like	What he likes for me	What I do
Appearance	Short hair	Long hair	Long hair
Career	Part-time	No work	Casual work
Hobbies	To learn a language	Tennis and cards	Tennis and cards
Time together	To spend it talking, cuddling and having sex sometimes	Doing jobs around the house or having sex	Do jobs around the house
Friends and family	See more of family and less of friends	See more of friends and less of family	Hardly see anyone
Spending money	Spend it on the house and nice dinners out	Spend it on holidays with friends	Save

having their needs met. Ironically, it is often the person whose needs are mostly being met who tires of the relationship and lacks commitment. In the example above, we might expect Marilyn's partner to begin to make less and less of an effort in the relationship, and then even lose his commitment to the relationship. Because if you allow yourself to become a doormat, you might become unattractive to the person you are trying to please.

Maintain a healthy sense of who you are

Understanding who you are, and what your needs are, ties in closely with your self-esteem. It is important to have interests and goals that are separate from your partner's. Being too dependent on your partner can be damaging and, in time, can erode your relationship. The telltale signs that this might be happening include the following:

1. You feel that you are often waiting for your partner.
2. You feel jealous of the time your partner is spending with other people.
3. You feel jealous of the time your partner is spending on their own pursuits.
4. You have difficulty making a decision that really only concerns you.
5. You feel you are often seeking your partner's reassurance about your relationship.

> *What I think makes our relationship work for us is that we don't live in each other's pockets.*
>
> Sally, 36 years

If you are in the throes of a new relationship and believe you are still in your bubble of new love, then you have to work especially hard on the necessary ground work to develop a successful relationship.

Tips for maintaining a healthy you

@ Don't make a habit of breaking commitments to others in order to accommodate your partner.
@ Ensure you maintain other friendships.
@ Keep up with your individual interests.
@ Be open with your partner about what you need from them.
@ Make specific requests.

It's up to you

Once you are aware of what your needs are, it is up to you to set about having them met. You cannot expect someone else to take on that responsibility. While you're at it, you can also look at what else you could change in your behaviour which would help you and, in turn, the relationship.

Working out what you, as an individual, can change in your relationship, is character building. Being able to change your own behaviour ties in closely with commitment. If you're committed to your partner, then doing something for him or her, even if it's not that big an issue for you, helps the relationship. Changing your own behaviour can also have a positive effect on the sequence of events that often leads to conflict. We call this the positive domino effect.

The positive domino effect

Did you ever play dominoes when you were a child? We remember standing them up close to each other in a curvy line and making one fall onto the next, and so on. What was left was a beautiful pattern of coloured dots facing upwards. Just as in dominoes, at any time in your relationship your behaviour can trigger a chain of events. The result can be either a positive outcome or a negative one.

Let's look at a few cases where one person's behaviour changing had a positive impact on their relationship.

Garry and Tina's story

Garry and Tina were in a long distance relationship. Often they didn't see each other for weeks at a time. Tina asked Garry to ring her every few days when he was away, and email her once a week to keep her up to date with his news. On the last trip, Tina was very upset when Garry only managed one brief email and irregular phone calls. Garry found writing a chore, although he knew it was important to Tina. Tina had made this request over and over, but it was only when he answered the question *What can **you** do differently to make the situation better?* did he give it a go.

Garry didn't promise the world to Tina in emails, but he did agree to change his behaviour. The positive domino effect surprised him. With a few brief emails, Tina was happier, which resulted in less stilted and more enjoyable phone calls.

> The positive domino effect = Changing a small part of your behaviour can effect a positive change in your relationship.

Stuart's story (52 years)

Stuart was having a hard time at work. Each morning he found facing the day difficult. His wife and kids would say: *Oh no, here we go again! You're so moody.* When Stuart came for help, his first wake up call came when he acknowledged that his family was not responsible for his lack of enjoyment at work. His second wake up call, was when he answered the question: *What can **you** do differently to make the situation better?*

Stuart found it helped to sit down to breakfast each morning with a smile and ask what his family's plans were for the day. He obviously also needed to work on his own unhelpful thoughts which were contributing to his depressed mood. But by merely changing his behaviour in this simple way, his mood improved a little (and so did his family's!).

What can you do differently?
Think of a current issue you're having with your partner.
@ What can you do differently to make the situation better?
@ What can you do to please your partner?

The importance of saying 'sorry'

You know that some of your behaviours irritate your partner. You also know deep down that you are neither a saint nor an angel. One way to maximise the chance of having a successful relationship is to learn to say 'I'm sorry'. For many people, who are perhaps too pig-headed, saying sorry is a near impossibility. This is a fundamental flaw that can potentially threaten the success of a relationship over time. This is because the person who cannot say sorry either thinks they're always right or has a serious problem communicating. Neither is very promising.

> **Be aware if either you or your partner has difficulty apologising. Successful relationships require both parties to accept responsibility and say 'I'm sorry'.**

How to develop self-assurance

Remember, having to rely on someone else to make you feel better decreases your self-worth and can often increase jealousy. Depending on someone to reassure you that you are a worthwhile person is a *short-term* solution. That is, you may feel better soon after being told that you are loved and wanted, but you will feel worse in the long run. By learning to resist the urge to seek reassurance in the short term, you will be helping yourself in the long run.

It is important to look at what you can do to develop a strong sense of feeling assured in yourself and your relationship. Let's look at Russell and Anita.

Russell and Anita's story

Russell came for help and brought a reluctant Anita with him. He loved her and she him. The problem was that Russell had become dependent on Anita reassuring him that she did love him. If she was late home from work, he assumed she didn't love him. If she was in a bad mood, he assumed she didn't love him. If she suggested that they do something separately, he waited for her to tell him that their relationship was over. After a year of asking Anita if she loved him, Russell was told in no uncertain terms to stop it. Anita decided she would no longer tell him when he asked. She had realised herself that her reassurances weren't helping.

It's easy to see what had been happening in their relationship:

1. Russell asks Anita if she loves him.

2. Increasing relief when she says she does.

3. Decreased ability to reassure himself and lowered self-esteem.

4. Increased dependence on that reassurance.

5. Increasing jealousy.

6. Becoming depressed and anxious about relationship.

7. The relationship is threatened.

So, if you often feel that you need to ask your partner to tell you over and over how they feel about you, the first step is to try hard to resist the urge to do so. The second step is to use clear thinking to change your self-defeating thoughts. Look at Russell's diary:

A ---- B ~~~~ C ·········· D ~~~~ E

Situation	Thoughts	Feelings/ Behaviour	New thoughts	New feelings/ Behaviour
Anita preoccupied and distant.	She's mad at me. She doesn't love me.	Anxious, self-conscious/ Ask her if she loves me.	She is really busy at work at the moment. Maybe it's nothing to do with me. She wouldn't be here if she didn't love me.	Calmer/ Don't ask.

By using clear thinking in this way, Russell was able to feel more confident about his relationship with Anita. This, in turn, improved the relationship remarkably for both of them.

Even if you don't feel it, behave in a self-assured way

Developing self-assurance is a slow process. Besides clear thinking, there are some other strategies which can be useful. One is to replace your pattern of behaviour with a positive action. At this time it's important to act in a self-assured way, even if you're not readily thinking in a self-assured way.

Let's look at another example – Sophie and Andrew.

Sophie and Andrew have an ongoing battle that goes something like this. They've been in a relationship for eighteen months, but live separately. Andrew doesn't like talking much about his work, especially at the end of the week. The more Sophie questions or demands information, the more Andrew withdraws and appears disinterested. Sophie falls into the faulty thinking trap of believing Andrew doesn't really respect her opinion. She then feels rejected and becomes needier and more demanding of his affection.

What Sophie first needed to do was to identify and challenge her negative thinking. Second, Sophie benefited from **behaving** in a confident, self-assured way. Initially she decided not to ask how Andrew's day had been, given that his usual response was 'too busy'. Instead, she immediately set about making plans for their evening together. She was bright and bubbly and carried on with her head held high. The more she acted in this way, the easier it was not to ask. She was pleasantly surprised to find that Andrew slowly started telling her more about his day.

So you can see that it is useful to learn how to replace your unhelpful patterns of behaviour with behaviour that resembles how you would *like to be* in those situations.

Jealousy – it just has to go

Jealousy is a problem that tends to occur in varying degrees in most relationships from time to time. It is a very destructive force in relationships, especially if it is often felt. People can be jealous about the time their partner spends with family or friends, or about contact with 'potential' partners. Feeling insecure often goes hand in hand with jealousy. We recommend that you aim to eliminate feeling jealous. But before you can do that, you need to understand where jealousy comes from.

When one person in a relationship is jealous, they're usually worried by the thought of losing their partner. These thoughts cause a strong negative emotion which is a mixture of feeling both fearful and angry at the same time. Unfortunately, possessive behaviour is an unpleasant by-product of jealousy. It comes in a number of forms, including 'checking up' on their partner, or questioning their partner's movements in an accusatory tone. If one person suspects that their partner is betraying them in some way, whether or not they actually are, then the person who feels jealous will have their antenna up searching for evidence to confirm their original worry. This sets up a vicious cycle, which can easily take on a life of its own. As the diagram below shows, what then happens is that the accused partner might become frustrated or annoyed and, in fact, keep information from their partner. This in turn can lead the jealous person to doubt themselves and feel more insecure about the relationship, and then the cycle goes on.

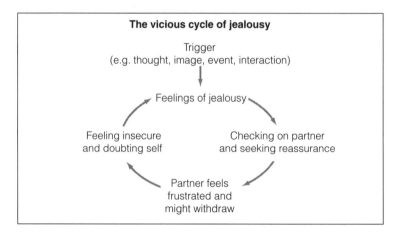

The vicious cycle of jealousy

Trigger
(e.g. thought, image, event, interaction)

Feelings of jealousy

Feeling insecure
and doubting self

Checking on partner
and seeking reassurance

Partner feels
frustrated and
might withdraw

Let's look at the types of thoughts that trigger jealousy and feeling insecure.

A ----------- B ~~~~~~~~~~ C

	trigger		cause	

Situation	Thoughts	Feelings/ Behaviour
At a party, boyfriend talking with others.	*He doesn't care about me. He's on the look-out for someone new.*	Sad, jealous, insecure/ Doesn't let boyfriend out of sight.
Girlfriend receives letter from ex-boyfriend.	*What if she wants him back?*	Worried, jealous/ Reads letter secretly.

Once the vicious cycle of jealousy is under way, the consequences can be damaging. If, in the above examples, the jealous person continues to allow themselves to be clingy or read private mail, then they are running the risk of establishing a self-fulfilling prophecy. Only a very tolerant person would put up with a clingy partner or one who secretly snoops through their personal property.

Being jealous has it roots in feeling insecure. How you think about yourself (your self-esteem) influences the type of thoughts you have. If you believe you are unworthy of someone's love and affection, or that you are no good, then you are more likely to find it difficult to handle your partner doing things without you or being friendly with other people. In fact, what you are fearing is being left alone.

> **Jealousy needs to be eliminated. Work on your self-doubt by challenging your unhelpful thinking.**

So how do you go about eliminating jealousy? As with other negative emotions, the first step is to identify your unhelpful thoughts by using clear thinking. This can often be a very confronting exercise but, nonetheless, a very useful one. As we have already outlined, it's best to complete the exercise after the fact. Think back to a situation when you felt jealous. To help identify your thoughts, ask yourself:

- What was I thinking at the time?
- If this is true, what does this say about me?
- If this is true, what does this say about us and our life?
- What is the worst thing that could happen?

Let's expand on one of the examples given above:

A ———————— **B** ~~~~~~~~~~ **C**

Situation	Thoughts	Feelings/ Behaviour
(trigger)	(cause)	
Girlfriend receives letter from ex-boyfriend.	*What if she wants him back?*	Worried, jealous/ Reads letter secretly.

- What was I thinking at the time? *What if she wants him back?*
- If this is true, what does this say about me? *I couldn't cope without her.*
- If this is true, what does this say about us and our life? *It's over.*
- What is the worst thing that could happen? *I would be miserable for the rest of my life.*

Once your thinking is expanded in this way, you can start to begin the process of challenging these thoughts using the questions we outlined in Chapter 6. Don't forget you're aiming for new thinking that is realistic, helpful and flexible.

- Where is the evidence for what I thought in B?
- What are the alternatives to what I thought in B?
- What is the likely effect on me of thinking this way?
- How would I advise a friend to think in the same situation?
- How would someone advise me?

In our example, the boyfriend was able to generate the following new thoughts:

I have no evidence to suggest that she wants to resume her relationship with her ex-boyfriend. It doesn't help me to worry about something that has not even been mentioned. In fact, she actually told me that she had received the letter, and is as loving as usual. If, at the end of the day, we did break up, I would be very sad but I would cope. I would have to work hard at keeping busy but, in time, I would probably find another girlfriend.

When did you feel jealous?

- Can you think of a time when you felt jealous?
- How could you rework your thinking to eliminate jealousy?

Given that jealousy stems from poor self-esteem, it is important to work on strategies to improve your self-esteem as well as challenge unhelpful thinking. These strategies include: developing your own interests, setting and achieving personal goals, developing and maintaining a good support network, taking responsibility for having your own needs met, and pampering yourself. At the end of the day, if you are in a relationship with someone who is very jealous and you are behaving appropriately, then it is up to them to do something about their jealousy.

Be wary if your new partner is often suspicious, possessive or very jealous of your behaviour. Over time, these feelings usually intensify.

Thinking clearly about sex

In all relationships, sexual issues arise at some stage. These issues include mismatched desire, concern over performance, or feeling unattractive. When these difficulties are tackled, there is often a fair amount of mind-reading and blaming taking place. When it comes to sexual difficulties, it is vital that you own your own problem. Only you can know how you are feeling, and therefore only you are responsible for initiating discussions about change.

Using clear thinking is the first step towards understanding why you are experiencing a problem.

Consider Paul and Vicky's situation. They came for help about their relationship. They had been together for eight years and had come to a point where they could no longer calmly discuss their sexual relationship. Paul was concerned that they were not having sex often enough. Vicky said she didn't want to have sex when they were at each other's throats most of the time.

Paul's thoughts were:

When we don't have sex, I think she doesn't want me – I take it as a total rejection.

Vicky's thoughts were:

It really hurts me that all he wants is sex. Even though we've fought all day, he wants to put all our other issues aside and just think of himself. Typical!

Eventually, they were able to challenge these thoughts that were keeping them 'stuck'.

Paul's new thoughts were:

I know Vicky loves me. We just view sex differently. She wants to feel happier about everything before she feels like having sex. I'll try to not sweep things under the carpet or take her rejection personally.

Vicky's new thoughts were:

Paul has always separated sex from our problems, as most men seem to be able to do. It doesn't mean he's being selfish or doesn't care about our problems.

You can see that clear thinking enabled them to think more realistically and less personally about their sex life. They obviously still had issues that needed to be resolved, but at least now they could enter discussions about these issues in a calmer state of mind. Such discussions would need to begin with Paul owning the problem of wanting sex more often than Vicky, and Vicky owning the problem of issues not being resolved.

IN BRIEF...

- ℮ Own your own problems. Don't wait for someone else to take responsibility for them.
- ℮ Ensuring that your own needs are met is not selfish.
- ℮ Maintain a healthy sense of who you are.
- ℮ Depending on someone else to reassure you erodes your self-esteem and your relationship in the end.
- ℮ It helps to act in a positive way.
- ℮ Learn to eliminate jealousy through clear thinking.

The lighter side......

Was there anything that first put you off your partner, but you now see as a strength?

I was worried that he was immature. I can see that he is just young at heart, and great with our children.

Lana, 31 years

I didn't really like the way she was so obsessed with being on time everywhere we went. Now I appreciate the fact that she is always reliable and that it has rubbed off on me.

Tom, 38 years

It seemed to me that she used to worry more about her friends than me. Now I know that she is wonderful at maintaining friendships, which has benefited both of us.

Michael, 42 years

I always used to tease him about his cleaning fetish. When I listen to my friends complaining about their husbands' failure to help around the house, I take it all back.

Susan, 36 years

I used to think he was really tight with his money. I now see that as a positive. We are now on track to get rid of a lot of debt and relax a little bit more.

Frances, 40 years

CHAPTER 9

OCEAN

Ideally you have now learnt some valuable skills for relying on yourself. We now want to introduce our OCEAN model of communication to illustrate how you can communicate more effectively with your partner.

The OCEAN model of communication

We have developed the OCEAN acronym as an easy way of remembering the steps needed to address a problem you might be having. This model can be applied to any problem you will face in your relationship.

What is OCEAN?
O = Own the problem
C = Change unhelpful thinking
E = Express the problem
A = Ask for help assertively
N = Negotiate

Now, let's take each step separately.

O = Own the problem

We have already discussed the reasons why it is vital that you own the problem you are experiencing. Although there are five parts to this model, this is the most important step. If you have not owned the problem, there is not much hope of a satisfying resolution.

C = Change unhelpful thinking

As we have discussed in the chapter on clear thinking, many of your distressing feelings can be put down to the unhelpful way you think at times. Remember Tony and Andrea, whom we introduced in the previous chapter. We learnt that Andrea was interpreting Tony's lack of help around the house as a sign of him not caring about her, only about their son. Ironically, Tony interpreted Andrea's nagging as a sign of her not loving their son. You can see that the problem can be easily complicated by such unhelpful interpretations. Once Andrea owned the problem, we could help her challenge her thoughts in the following way:

A ----- B ~~~~ C ·········· D ~~~~ E

Situation	Thoughts	Feelings/ Behaviour	New thoughts	New feelings/ Behaviour
Tony not helping with housework.	*He only cares about Saxon. I'm just the slave.*	Angry, resentful/ Sulk or yell.	*He really does love Saxon and housework is the furthest thing from his mind. We will need to sit down and discuss what to do about my problem.*	Less angry/More willing to talk calmly and explore options and make requests.

E = Express the problem

Once you have owned the problem and addressed any hidden unhealthy thoughts, you are then in a position to express your problem to your partner. Remember, without assuming that the other person is responsible for your happiness, and without assuming that their behaviour means they do not love you, the expression will be far less of an attack. To illustrate the difference, look at the following comparisons:

Healthy vs unhealthy expression
Issue = Andrea not wanting to be solely responsible for housework

1. Expression of issue without ownership of problem

   You are so slack. Why do I have to do everything? I'm sick of this!

2. Expression of issue with underlying unhelpful thoughts

   If you really loved me, you would help me, not treat me like a slave!

3. Expression of issue **with** ownership and **without** unhelpful thoughts

   I am very upset because I believe I am doing all the housework.

You can see that the third expression is the most likely to achieve what Andrea wants, and that is help with **her** problem. With ownership and without the unhelpful thoughts, her message is clear and far more inviting. Even though the problem of the housework is still unresolved, they are now in a position to move towards making some joint decisions.

The importance of listening
We want to take a moment to highlight the important skill of listening. There is no point in owning the problem, and then

learning to express yourself well, if your partner is not prepared to listen to you. To really hear the other person you need to listen without interrupting. The real test of whether you have heard the other person is to be able to repeat to them their words and feelings. For example:

> *You said you are very upset because you believe you are doing all the housework. Is that right?*

It may sound very theoretical to 'listen' in this way, but how many times have you all assumed you have been heard and in fact you have not? In addition, how many times have you messed up what you were trying to say and only realised it when someone attempted to repeat what you had just said? By attempting some sort of formal listening exercise, you can reduce the chances of these two mistakes happening. If your partner refuses to ever listen, then the problems go beyond communication difficulties. At the end of this chapter we suggest what to do when you hit a brick wall like this.

A = Ask for help assertively

One of the hardest things for a lot of people to do is to ask for help. No doubt you would prefer for someone to know just what you want and do it for you. But that would rely on the skill of mind-reading and, as we have said before, mind-reading is a no-no. How often have you heard or thought any of these expressions?

> *You know I hate it when you leave your clothes on the floor.*

> *If you don't know why I'm upset and what to do about it, then things are worse than I thought!*

> *Why should I have to ask him/her to help me around the house? It's his/her house too!*

These three statements all indicate the same problem. They are obviously said by someone who is upset. They all assume the listener knows that they are upset and should know how to fix things. None of them ask specifically for help. Compare them with the following three statements, making a specific request, which have been reworded:

I'm pretty angry that, despite my nagging, your clothes are still on the floor. Do you think you could try harder to remember to hang them up at night?

I'm upset that you didn't remember our anniversary. We need to do something to acknowledge the date because I don't want to be disappointed again.

*It would be easier for me if we worked out who is responsible for what as far as the chores go, because I don't want to keep asking you to help me as I think of the chores as **ours**, not **mine.***

You can see that in these last three statements, emotion is still expressed. We suggest that you acknowledge your feelings and politely make requests. Everybody gets upset and everybody gets angry. But when you are trying to communicate how you feel and what you want, you need to be specific and ask for help.

Be assertive

When asking for help, it is important to be assertive. Assertiveness can be defined as telling someone the truth in an appropriate manner. By *an appropriate manner*, we mean that you do not see yourself as superior to others, which can lead to aggressive behaviour. Neither does it mean that you see yourself as inferior to others, which can lead to passive or unassertive behaviour. It just means that you see yourself as equal to others.

To *lie* about your own thoughts and feelings is also being unassertive. By lying about how you really think and feel, you are waiving your right to be understood, accepted and helped by others. You are also giving away your right to be angry or resentful. No-one can correct a wrong, or address your needs, if they are hidden.

Clearly the first three statements above are unassertive. On the other hand, each of the second group of statements is assertive, and makes a clear request. A general rule of thumb is to use *I* statements in your request.

Starting a discussion with 'You...' inevitably causes the other person to become defensive and start a fight, or refuse to talk. But starting a discussion with an *I* statement increases the likelihood that the other person will listen to whatever problem *you have*.

N = Negotiate

Negotiation is needed in all relationships at some stage. If you and your partner can't agree on something, then you both have to sit down and work out a solution that is agreeable to you both. In the OCEAN model, negotiation is the final step if your request for change is met with opposition. Before we explain more about this process, we always like to set some ground rules for negotiation.

Ground rules

@ Try not to use your bed as a centre for the hearing of disputes.

@ Try not to have a serious discussion over a meal.

@ Try not to have a serious discussion just before one person is leaving the house, or just after they return.

@ Try not to talk about personal issues in front of a child.

@ Try to set up a time which is relatively convenient to both parties and briefly say what you would like to address beforehand so that the other person can think about the issue.

Once you have found a suitable time and place (not easy, we admit), you can start attempting to resolve the problem.

In all relationships it is important to be able to air your grievances. Keeping in mind the ground rules mentioned above, set up a time and place for your grievance session. If you can't agree on an issue, then you need to put in the necessary effort to find a solution. We believe that writing down issues helps tremendously. Brainstorming is the first step once the problem has been defined. We recommend using our 'Framework for making choices' at this point.

How to make an informed decision

It's helpful to have a framework for making decisions to solve problems in your relationship. When you are faced with difficult decisions, procrastinating doesn't help. In the end, it only makes the decision-making process more difficult.

In our practice we use a standard framework for making choices. This framework is useful in all areas of your life when a decision needs to be made. The framework includes eight questions. The first six questions get you to the point of making the choice happen. The final two questions are what you need to ask yourself once you have put into practice the choice you made. These look at whether you are happy with your choice. If you are not, then it is a matter of reworking the previous steps.

This method of formally making choices encourages rational, objective thinking. It means that you have to think a lot about the possible consequences of certain outcomes. In this sense, it is a very deliberate choice. Using the framework helps negotiation tremendously. Even if the final choice is not your own preference, as a couple you will have settled on an option on which you both agree. Further, there will be a clear reason why a certain alternative has been chosen. Finally, there is the opportunity to review the outcome of the decision down the track.

Framework for making choices

1. What is the problem you are experiencing? (Be specific.)

_____

_____

2. How many possible solutions can you suggest for this problem? (Don't worry about how ridiculous they might seem.)

_____

_____

3. What are the positives and negatives of each of these possible solutions?

_____

_____

_____

4. Which looks best to you? (Which has the most positives?)

_____

_____

5. If you used this solution, what would the consequences be?

_____

_____

6. What steps do you need to take to try this solution out?

_____

_____

7. Once you have done it, are you happy with the outcome?

_____

_____

8. If you are not happy with your choice, are there any little changes that would improve the outcome? If not, go back to step 2 and rework the steps.

_____

_____

Applying the OCEAN model to sexual issues

Accepting responsibility for problems can actually lead to increased self-esteem and greater intimacy in relationships. Nowhere is this more clearly illustrated than in a couple's sexual relationship. Many people assume that their partner should know how to please them. If they don't know, then it is concluded that there is no hope. But, if there is one place where mind-reading is absolutely useless, it's in the bedroom!

Couples who seek counselling are often best helped by developing insight into *their own problems*. If you are not satisfied with your sexual relationship, then *it is your problem.* That is not to say that it is your fault. Rather, it is up to you to accept responsibility for getting the problem resolved. Conversely, if your partner accepts responsibility for their feelings of dissatisfaction, no doubt you would be more likely to help in the problem's resolution.

Different ways of approaching Sam's problem

Consider the following approach to addressing a simple issue:

Sam: *You never want to just cuddle me anymore. You are too busy with the children or the housework, or talking on the phone, to even stop and give me a kiss hello.*

Maggie: *You're right. I am too busy doing everything around here. I can't add giving you a kiss or cuddle every five minutes to the list. I'd never have any time to scratch myself!*

Now using the OCEAN model Sam could have handled *his problem* this way.

Sam: *Gosh I miss kissing and cuddling you! Do you miss it too?* (Owning the problem and expressing it.)

Maggie: *Sure, but I have so much to do now that the last thing on my mind is doing any of that stuff.*

Sam: *Yeah, life has really changed. I wonder if we could think of ways to enjoy one minute with each other. I know we do it for the kids. I think it would be nice if we could try to do it for us too.* (Asking for help.)

Maggie: *It's a nice thought. I don't see it becoming a reality though. Maybe if you helped to pack away those toys, there would be less for me to do.*

Sam: *Let's just give it a go. I'll start to pack up the toys and let's see if we can get to bed a bit earlier.* (Negotiating.)

In the first example Sam was accusatory and not taking any responsibility for something which was bugging him. Maggie wasn't worrying about the lack of cuddling going on. Therefore it was not up to her to initiate attempts to resolve the issue. In the second example, Sam owned the problem, and made suggestions as to how to address the issue. If there were unhelpful thoughts which were causing him to be particularly unhappy, he would need to challenge them before expressing his problem.

Which approach do you think would be more likely to lead to a better outcome for Sam?

Sam's issue was relatively easy to tackle. But when more personal details of your sexual wants and needs are an issue for you, it can all become too difficult. Whether you're feeling unattractive, or you want to address your desire for more oral sex or the use of sex aids, the same rules of the OCEAN model apply. By following the steps, it is amazing how much easier it becomes to discuss really personal issues. If you are owning the problem and are then asking your partner if they can help you with it, then the difference between asking for a one-minute cuddle and asking for something new in bed is minimised.

Hitting a brick wall

What do you do when you have owned your problem, you have attempted to let your partner know how you feel about something, but your partner doesn't budge? It is now time for you to make some decisions. Using our 'Framework for making choices' (p. 123) may help here. For example, if you and your partner cannot agree on a resolution to an issue, or if your partner just won't talk about it, or won't listen, you need to explore your options. These options could include couple counselling or even leaving the relationship (if the issue is divisive enough). Remember, when you are considering these choices, you need to not only examine the positive and negative aspects, but also the consequences of each of them. You also need to look at the necessary steps for carrying out the chosen option. Using such a deliberate method for making decisions reduces the chance of impulsiveness and regrets.

You might reach the point where you decide to leave, even if you have been committed all along. When this happens, it is a very sad day because you have to accept that it is beyond your control. Commitment is a two-way path and, if there's only one of you on it, then there is no relationship. If you believe you have exhausted all your options for trying to involve your partner, then you can walk away knowing that you tried everything to salvage your relationship.

IN BRIEF...
- **O** = Own the problem
- **C** = Change unhelpful thinking
- **E** = Express the problem
- **A** = Ask for help assertively
- **N** = Negotiate

The lighter side.....

What makes your relationship work for you?

We give each other space to pursue our own interests, which we call 'a life-giving consideration'. What's really important though, is that we take an interest in what the other is doing.

Alexei, 41 years

We try to follow the advice: don't go to bed when you're angry with each other.

David, 36 years

We try to have a good laugh together at least once a week.

Joanna, 29 years

She's my best friend and I'm hers.

Daniel, 31 years

We really respect each other.

Louisa, 30 years

My mother always said, 'Be kind to each other.'

Catherine, 44 years

I love the effort she makes for me. I'm learning to do the same for her.

Joel, 32 years

10 | Nothing stays the same

Life throws up many challenges. You face these challenges as individuals and as couples. How you and your partner accommodate these changes, whether they are wanted or unwanted, will determine whether or not you remain on your relationship path. There are many possible upheavals you could all face at any time. The main aim of this chapter is to outline some strategies to help you deal with the changes in life. As you read through some of the likely changes and the strategies for coping with these events, it is worthwhile keeping in mind the following five lines:

For better for worse
For richer for poorer,
In sickness and in health,
To love and to cherish,
as long as we both shall live.

Not everyone marries. Of those who do marry, not everyone will use these marriage vows, but if they stop and look at these lines, most people would agree with the sentiment.

The changes in life

As we discussed in Chapter 7, certain events in life affect your relationship. Let's now look briefly at a few examples of both positive and negative events that you might face during your life.

Marriage

In a book about relationships it would seem a little odd not to talk about how marriage or entering into a de facto relationship initially affects you. Even though it's common for couples to live together before marriage, many people have told us that something changes between them when they actually marry.

Living with someone for the first time can be a huge shock to the system, even if you do love them. It's very hard to be tolerant all the time of each other's ways and habits. Accepting that someone else might do something differently to you is part of the steep learning curve required to survive living together. Adapting to how someone else lives can take time and requires skilful negotiation. A little thing that would usually not be an issue in separate households can become a great source of irritation. In the bigger scheme of things, these little irritations don't really mean much. Learning to think differently is one way to become more tolerant and more accepting.

> We'd been living together for four years before we decided to get married. Wanting to have children was the catalyst for going ahead with it. I was surprised that I felt different when we actually did marry – something clicked. I think it has to do with the fact that I stood up in front of my family and friends, and made public my commitment.
>
> Liz, 32 years

> **A relationship's success is partly determined by the partners' ability to accommodate change.**

Part of making the adjustment to marriage means getting used to something new. Whether you lived with your parents, a flatmate, or on your own before you married, getting used to something different can be tricky. At first you might be lonely, especially if you're used to a busy household, or you might feel like a fish out of water if you have moved cities. Whatever your specific set of circumstances, keep your expectations flexible because it takes at least one year to get used to any major change.

> *I got married when I was 25 years old. I'd lived with a very close girlfriend for several years and, just before my wedding, I moved home for a few months. It took a while to get used to my new life, as I went from a very busy house to a very quiet one.*
>
> Stephanie, 29 years

Parenthood

People the world over will agree that parenthood presents one of the biggest challenges in life. No amount of reading or listening to friends' advice can prepare you for the shock a new baby brings to your life. Whether the pregnancy was planned or not will also have a great influence on how a couple deals with the news. A baby affects both individuals as well as the relationship between these individuals. Every couple will experience the transition to parenthood in their own way. Some will say that a baby has brought them closer. Others say that parenthood marked the beginning of the end of the relationship. Most people fall somewhere in between. As is always the case, the individual's expectations greatly affect how that person will cope with the transition. The more unrealistic the expectations, the greater the difficulty when the baby finally arrives.

Let's look at the individual experience first.

As a woman...

Some women are aware of being pregnant as soon as conception occurs. For others, it takes a while. However long it takes, a woman does change forever once she becomes pregnant. Physically, she might feel tired and nauseous. She might have sensitive breasts. Her sex drive might increase or decrease. Emotionally, she might be excited and scared. She might be preoccupied with the pregnancy. She might be afraid of hurting her unborn child. She will no doubt be nervous about the birth.

Labour brings on a new challenge – both emotionally and physically. As a result, the weeks and months following the birth will be affected by hormones settling, stitches healing and breasts adjusting to their new role. Of course we cannot forget that there is also a new baby to look after. There might be many tears – both of happiness and frustration.

> *Nothing could have prepared me for the absolute and total shock of giving birth and then caring for this little, helpless thing. I read a lot of books, but until you actually do it, it's hard to imagine.*
>
> Sarah, 31 years

How much does the new mother think about her partner's needs? The answer is – probably not much at all. Between her physical and emotional recovery, and the adaptation to her new role as mother, there is not much time to worry about her partner. Does this change to her relationship worry her? Probably not much. In the first few months, she is so busy and preoccupied with being a mother that the last thing on her mind is how her partner is coping. Their sexual relationship is probably the furthest thing from her mind.

As each baby grows, the mother's focus widens, and the relationship comes into view again. At this moment, some concern might set in as she realises the amount of time she has spent apart from her partner, and how long it has been since they last had sex. Her inclination might be to address the issue quickly, or it might be to ignore the problem altogether. How she copes with the realisation that their relationship has changed will depend on the expectations she had, and on how her partner is coping.

Each milestone reached by the child creates a new set of challenges for the mother. Starting school, puberty, adolescence, leaving home, and the children themselves having children, cause different emotions and reactions in different women. Each of these phases also has an effect on the relationship the woman has with her partner.

As a man...

A man also experiences changes in his life from the moment a pregnancy is announced. There might be anxiety, excitement and confusion. Without the experience of pregnancy itself, the man has to sit it out and wait for his child's birth. This waiting can be difficult for him, especially if his reaction is interpreted by his partner as one of indifference to her. He may have misgivings about sex during pregnancy for fear of hurting the baby. Sometimes his fear can be seen by his partner as being a loss of desire for her.

The birth itself is an amazing experience for some men, and a real turn-off for others. Women can have trouble understanding the reaction their men have, which can be a source of arguments down the track. We have certainly talked to a number of men who felt differently about their partners after watching the birth experience. Some said that they had a new found respect for their partner after seeing what she went through. Others could not get the grisly image of the birth out of their minds and found it very difficult to approach their partners sexually afterwards.

> *I was scared for her and for me. I had planned to just keep close to her head, but I looked down at the wrong moment and saw her tear. I have found it hard to have sex because I can't forget that sight. It's hard for both of us now.*
>
> Marty, 39 years

> *I loved her before. I was proud of her before. But after seeing what she and her body can do – I am in awe of her.*
>
> Edward, 29 years

Life with a new baby is a confusing time for many men. They can feel like the third wheel, wondering where they fit in. Feeling left out can lead to resentment which, in turn, can lead some men to question their commitment. This doesn't happen overnight; it is a gradual process and usually reflects unresolved issues from before.

> *My wife breast-fed our son for the first twelve months. I must admit I did feel a little left out at times.*
>
> John, 35 years

> *Being a father is the best thing in my life. I just love the days I am at home with my children.*
>
> Scott, 35 years

Overall, most men tend to become more and more involved as their baby grows. Finding their feet as fathers takes a little while, but brings new confidence and new contentment. It's normal for a man to feel he is lagging a bit behind his partner in the confidence stakes; she has a nine months' head start, and usually clocks up a lot more time with the baby in those early years. A few men remain anxious or irritated about having children, and grieve for life as they had previously known it. They tend to resist becoming involved with their children and, unfortunately, everyone misses out in the end.

> The first two years was a very difficult time for me. To be honest I don't like the baby stage when they don't really do anything. It is getting easier now and I couldn't imagine life without them.
>
> Colin, 34 years

> If I could turn back the clock, knowing what I do now, I would have preferred not to have had children.
>
> Robert, 35 years

As a couple...

One of the most common consequences of starting a family is that the couple has less time to spend together. Those sleep-ins, the Sunday brunch, the impromptu movie, the late night walk – all vanish at first. This reduction in the time you spend together is normal, but does need to be addressed. First, how you feel about this loss needs to be discussed. Second, couples need to learn to set up regular times to be with each other, to have sex, and to discuss family issues. Sure, these meetings are not spontaneous, but they can be romantic, and are crucial to your survival as a couple. Also, work out a system so that both of you get some time alone to pursue your own interests. Finally, both of you need to make sure that your thinking is helpful and realistic. The important thing is the way in which you think about your situation. Aim for something like this: *We have to expect our lives will change when we have children. We won't be able to do as many things as easily or as spontaneously as before, but that doesn't mean we won't enjoy ourselves. We are happy with our decision to have children. We are moving into a different phase of our life and, in time, we will find out what works best for us.* It's important therefore, to keep the

> We try most Friday evenings to watch a video together once the kids are in bed. It's something we both look forward to and gives us the opportunity to just be with each other.
>
> Cathy, 33 years

lines of communication open, and put safeguards in place to ensure that everyone is having their needs met most of the time.

> After children are born, set up regular dates to see each other, to discuss family issues and, believe it or not, to have sex.

As your children grow up, your relationship is regularly put to the test. There are many potential triggers for conflict – discipline, education, and managing careers and family roles, just to mention a few. Each time a new challenge is thrown at you, you need to address the issues before they become huge problems. Let's look at James and Maureen's dilemma. It looked simple, but created a great deal of tension between them.

James and Maureen's story

When they first came for help James and Maureen couldn't agree on a number of issues. They had been married for 25 years and had three children. Two of the children were still at home while studying at university.

Maureen: *I would like the two of us to go on an overseas holiday for a few months. We've both worked hard and only now can we afford to go. James wants to wait because he thinks we still need to be at home to look after the kids. I think the kids are old enough to manage on their own. We were married by their age. I'm sick of putting everything on hold. We're not getting any younger.*

James: *I just worry that something might go wrong and we wouldn't be here. I suppose I've always been more protective. Nothing has ever happened, but it's a big step. I would like to go away, but I'd like to leave it until they have all left home and are settled in their own lives.*

The first problem Maureen and James had to acknowledge is that they have very different personalities, which greatly influences their views on the ability of their adult children to cope without them. Maureen had always been more relaxed and allowed her children to learn from their mistakes. James, on the other hand, was more cautious and tried to pre-empt any problems for his children. When they explored their differences, it was obvious that many of their fights over the years were triggered by their different beliefs about parenting. Up until now, the usual pattern of resolving these differences was to sweep the differences under the carpet. At times it was easy to do because Maureen was a stay-at-home mum during the children's younger years and tended to tackle more of the day-to-day issues herself. Now, however, the issue they were facing was not so easy to ignore.

The second problem concerned James's level of anxiety about letting go and taking risks. He described himself as always having been the nervous type. He needed to work on this individually, because there was a very real chance that if he didn't, they would never go on an overseas holiday. The reasons that prevented them going would just change.

Only then, after considering all of their options, could they make a decision together about the holiday. In the end they compromised and planned two shorter trips.

James and Maureen's issue of an overseas holiday was the culmination of many years of failing to address the differences in their personalities, and in their beliefs about parenting.

As a step-parent...

Being a step-parent can be particularly difficult and requires careful and thoughtful preparation. When people enter into a relationship where children are involved, they often fail to realise that, in time, differences in parenting style can easily erode the relationship.

I thought that my second husband was 'it' for me from the start. Now after ten years of marriage and being a step-mother I would have to say that I never envisaged the strain that our relationship would have to bear because of the frequent interference from his ex-wife. I don't think she has ever come to terms with the fact that he left her for another woman and he finds it difficult to be firm with her.

Carole, 48 years

Setting ground rules ahead of time can help ease the process. Taking time to allow the relationship with your step-children to build is essential. Don't expect to **feel** the same about your step-children as you do about your own children. But a consistent parenting approach is crucial. It is therefore necessary for both of you to agree on how the nonbiological parent will discipline their step-children.

We strongly encourage step-parents to talk to other parents in the same position, read current literature, attend seminars and seek counselling if needed. The most successful step-families we have seen are those who have had realistic expectations about the potential difficulties, are flexible, and have not shied away from the tricky issues.

> *I met my husband a few years after he and his wife separated. He has three children with her and two with me. Even though there have been some rough patches with his children, we all get on remarkably well.*
> *Thinking back, what has really helped is that I was never 'the other woman'.*
>
> Hannah, 39 years

> *My wife and I both have children from our first marriages, but none together. My children live with their mother and my wife's children live with us. We end up spending a lot of our time arguing about parenting issues. She thinks I'm too hard on her children and I think she isn't tough enough. Over the years, as the children have gone through adolescence, our differences have become more obvious. Unfortunately, the little time we do have alone on alternate weekends is often spoiled by a lingering argument about the children. I would hate to see my second marriage end too.*
>
> Derek, 45 years

> *I find it really hard to bite my tongue when I see my wife's 16-year-old son treating her disrespectfully. But I have learnt my lesson – it's best to keep right out otherwise she turns on me.*
>
> Frank, 48 years

Be a team player

The challenges resulting from becoming parents often create conflict around the issue of **who is the worst off?** When couples attempt to answer this question, the team is split. One person will think that their daily life is more difficult. But they are not living in their partner's shoes, and this line of thinking prevents the couple working as a team.

How does it help the relationship to compare a mother who works part-time outside the home with a father who might work full-time in a stressful job? This is a very difficult question and one that is sometimes hard to let go. Such competition breeds resentment and splits the team. The truth is that your partner **does not know** how hard life is for you, nor do you **know** how hard it is for them. No-one can ever feel someone else's physical or emotional pain. Rather than trying to win the competition over the problems you have, try challenging the thoughts along the following lines.

A ----- B ~~~~ C ·········· D ~~~~ E

Situation	Thoughts	Feelings/ Behaviour	New thoughts	New feelings/ Behaviour
Man comes home to an upset wife.	*Here she goes again. Little does she know how easy she has it – only working two days a week! I've had such a bad day, the last thing I need is to comfort her.*	Angry, resentful/ Doesn't talk.	*She seems really upset. Maybe her day has been bad. Just because it's not the same as my day, doesn't mean it wasn't bad.*	Less angry/More willing to listen and help.

> **You can't be a team player if you're competing for points.**

Once this man's competitive thoughts were challenged, a resolution for his wife's problem automatically became more likely and they could begin working as a team. Letting go of asking: *Who is the worse off?* is certainly one place to start changing your behaviour for the benefit of the relationship. What we emphasise to our clients is that they have a **choice** as to whether or not they go down the path of comparing who is worse off. We recommend that, instead, they listen to each other about their respective hardships and try to help the other out.

> *I am working part-time, looking after two children and the home, not to mention the dog. My partner finds his job pretty stressful and not that enjoyable. When we're both tired at the end of the day, we easily slip into making snide comments to each other about how hard our day has been. I hate the way he thinks his day is over when he walks in the door. I usually sulk.*
>
> Christine, 40 years

How to be a team player

- Don't point score.
- Challenge any unhelpful thinking.
- Don't ask who is worse off.
- Listen to each other.
- Acknowledge that each of your jobs has difficult aspects.
- Brainstorm ways to help each other.
- Suggest ways for the other person to help you out.
- Make specific requests.

The empty nest

As children grow older, relationships weather many ups and downs. One common problem is that couples no longer set goals for themselves as individuals, or as couples. Children can easily become the primary focus and once the children have left home, an obvious void appears. The *empty nest*, as this void has been referred to, can be a problem in relationships, especially if one person feels it more than the other. The term is typically used to describe the feelings many women experience after their children have left home. But men can feel it too. The 'symptoms' include not knowing what to do; feeling lonely, flat or depressed; and experiencing a loss of direction. A full and busy life is quite suddenly replaced by a life of less activity. The empty nest syndrome is perhaps more typical of the generation of mothers of today's adults; most of the current generation of mothers with young children will probably be employed when their children leave home. The gap then won't be quite as noticeable. It is a totally normal reaction to another major change in one's life. Sometimes it's necessary to seek professional help if this reaction continues for some time.

A woman might also experience a taste of the empty nest syndrome when her youngest child starts school. Again, this is a perfectly normal reaction because she is experiencing a major change.

To ward off the empty nest syndrome you need to ensure that you develop both individual and couple interests. In Chapter 15, we have a yearly goals exercise that you might also find helpful. For now, ask yourself the following questions:

How to prevent yourself from living in an empty nest

@ What activities did you like to do as an individual before you had children?

@ What activities did you like to do as a couple before you had children?

@ How many of these activities do you still do now?

@ Which ones would you like to do more frequently?

@ Is there anything else you would like to do?

@ What steps do you need to take to increase your individual and couple activities?

How to manage life events

Whatever the issue, it is important that both of you work out what is needed to maintain a healthy sense of control. What we suggest is that both the individual who is experiencing the problem and their partner think about how they can manage the situation together. Again this is where seeing yourself as a team can be to your advantage. For example, if the issue is that one of you is infertile, it is far healthier to see it as 'our' problem. Apportioning blame only splits the team.

We believe that the best way to manage change is to develop a formula that is specific to the problem at hand. Our 'Formula for managing life events' is a good starting point, especially for those events that affect one of you more than the other. If the problem is short-lived then the plan will look slightly different to a plan for an ongoing condition. Remember, work towards being able to accommodate change because it will determine to a large extent how successful your relationship will be.

Formula for managing life events

The basic components for developing your own formula as a couple include the following:

1. What does my partner need from me to help him/her manage the issue he/she is facing?
   - Provide support, encouragement.
   - Attend appointments if necessary.
   - Read current literature.
   - Be available to listen if asked.
   - To listen over and over if necessary.
   - Resist problem solving.
   - Resist criticising.
   - Praise any gain, no matter how small.

2. What do we need to do as a couple?
   - Read current literature.
   - Talk openly about what is happening for both of us.
   - Listen to each other.
   - Make requests of each other.
   - Develop a support network.
   - Consider all options.

3. What do I need to do as an individual to manage the issue I'm facing?
   - Identify expectations; are they realistic?
   - Change my unhelpful thoughts.
   - Seek professional help if needed.
   - Seek individual support if needed.

Let's now look at some other life events that we know can strain even the best of relationships. The 'Formula for managing life events' can also be applied to these examples.

Retirement and redundancy

When one person is faced with a career change – whether it's by choice, by retirement, or by redundancy – they will go through a

major transition and they may experience some kind of identity crisis.

If it were an unwanted change, they could have a tough time as they adjust to the loss. In that way, their feelings are similar to someone who is grieving. At first they might find it hard to believe. What sometimes happens is that the concern or worry that the person feels is often felt by their partner too. Since a job is a very defining characteristic for a person, especially a man, in our society, their self-esteem usually takes a pounding. Similarly, someone who is declared bankrupt may experience the same kind of blow to their self-esteem. In these situations, the relationship tends to cop the brunt of the person's self-doubt. You know that you can be rotten to your partner in a way you would never be to a friend. Why? Because you take them for granted, you relax your standards, you have bad habits. Also, your partner is less likely to end the relationship since they have a lot at stake, just as you do.

> *I was made redundant in my early fifties. Even though I had planned to retire at 55 years, it still came as a huge shock. I found myself at a loss and it was hard not to let it get me down.*
>
> Ken, 55 years

> *My husband was made redundant about twelve months ago. He decided to set up his own business doing contract work that has been slow to get started. I find having him at home a lot of the time very difficult. I feel guilty when I want to get out and do my own thing. A lot of the time I feel resentful. I just wish he'd get out more.*
>
> Bronwyn, 52 years

Issues about leaving the workplace can be extremely sensitive because, first, no-one knows what the other person really feels in that situation, and second, no-one knows what the other person thinks about themselves in relation to that situation. Many unresolved issues and insecurities can be brought to the surface when such a change occurs. Often individual counselling is needed to process the person's thoughts and feelings.

Infertility

Infertility often comes as a huge shock. When they are young most people don't give much thought to whether or not they will be able to have children. The sad fact is that many people who want to have children will not be able to do so. There are many combinations here: the woman is diagnosed as being infertile, the man is diagnosed as being infertile, or no abnormality is detected in either partner. Again such a life event can really rock the best of relationships. What's important is maintaining the team approach and being there to support each other. Counselling is certainly recommended. Often individual work needs to be done if one person is having a particularly hard time or is blaming themselves. Unfortunately, it's often not recognised that a time of grieving is normal to allow that person to move on. It's okay to cry, and to think of how things might have been. That's all part of resolving the loss.

Susan and Kevin's story illustrates the ups and downs a couple can experience when faced with infertility.

Susan and Kevin's story

Susan: *We had been together for several years before actually deciding to get married. We wanted to start a family. Kevin was happier to wait a few more years before actually trying to get pregnant but, as I was 34, I wanted to start as soon as we could. I've always loved children and all my life have longed for the day I'd become a mother. Our relationship was solid and I felt that the time was right.*

We began trying seven years ago. When I wasn't pregnant in the first month, I was naturally disappointed. As each month passed, I became more and more obsessed about having a baby. I also became more and more depressed. After about twelve months we began a series of investigations. All seemed okay, so we tried for a few more months. My impatience was overwhelming. It was hard to think about much else. Initially we tried fertility drugs, and when nothing happened we decided to go on the IVF program. We've now been on that for about five years in total. I'm sad to say that I have never had a pregnancy despite a number of embryos being put back each time. We're now not sure what our next step will be.

At times our relationship has been difficult. I am guilty of taking out my hurt on Kevin. I don't mean to, but it just happens. I'm also not the fun, easy-going person I once was, as I feel totally drained by the whole process. I worry that one day he might get sick of it all, and walk out. If we survive this, I think we can survive anything.

Kevin: *Trying to have a baby has certainly been a long hard slog. I know that it's something Susan wants so much and it really is hard not to be able to give it to her. For me, if it doesn't happen, then that's the way it is for us. I've tried to be as supportive as I can, especially when she is actually going through the procedure, but we've certainly had some bleak moments.*

Menopause

Menopause is a huge transition for many women. As with pregnancy, women have to undergo enormous physical and emotional changes when they reach menopause. How a woman thinks about herself and what menopause means to her will also be unique to the woman. Some women feel very depressed as they equate their ability to reproduce with their self-worth. Other women are pleased that they can say goodbye to periods and no longer worry about getting pregnant. Men will also react in different ways to the knowledge that their partner is going through menopause. Their reaction will also be very much driven by what they think about menopause. Some men don't notice. Other men can react negatively, putting down every disagreement or argument to the fact that their partner is going through menopause.

When I started going through menopause I felt down and found the whole thing difficult to cope with. Luckily for me, my husband was very understanding. He just listened and tried to cheer me up.

May, 56 years

It seems that every time I get upset about something, my husband blames it on the menopause. It might be having some effect on my moods, but it certainly doesn't excuse his inconsiderate behaviour.

Beth, 51 years

Chronic illness

With chronic illness we recommend the same approach as outlined in our 'Formula for managing life events' (p. 141). Even though the illness may only physically affect one of you, the relationship does need to undergo a period of adjustment. Reassessing each other's needs on an ongoing basis is important.

As we said before, it's impossible to imagine anyone else's pain, so you shouldn't try. This basic inability to actually feel someone else's pain leads to different problems for the person in pain and for the partner. If you are in pain, you can feel let down by your partner because they don't understand what you are going through. If you are the partner of someone in pain you can feel frustrated by the chronicity of the problem and the depression which may result.

It was really hard at first when my partner was diagnosed with chronic fatigue syndrome. I had started a new job, which meant long days. She was at home not doing much. I felt under a lot of pressure to be there for her. We also had to restrict our social life, which was frustrating at times. What helped was seeing her doctors too. We were then much more open about what was happening.

Adam, 37 years

My husband suffered a head injury a few years ago. He hasn't been quite the same since. It helped me greatly when I attended a support group at the doctor's suggestion.

Julie, 46 years

Depression and anxiety

In our practice we see many people who suffer from depression or anxiety. These conditions undoubtedly have a huge impact on the individual's relationship. Depression can hit anyone at any stage in their life. A depressive episode may coincide with periods of great stress and change. Such triggers might be the birth of a baby, as in postnatal depression, or experiencing a personal trauma. When someone is depressed, the way in which they view their world, themselves and others is usually very negative. They might find it hard to see the bright side of things, and to enjoy their regular activities. A person who is depressed withdraws and usually finds it hard to be motivated or make decisions. Living with someone like this can be extremely difficult and frustrating. The dynamics of the relationship certainly change, even if only for a short period of time. We certainly recommend that the couple attend counselling together and read relevant literature to increase their understanding of the condition.

With anxiety disorders – such as panic disorder with agoraphobia, and social phobia – the relationship can also be put to the test. Anxiety conditions can be extremely debilitating, especially where the person relies heavily on their partner for support to help them feel safe in certain situations. With panic disorder, for example, a person might find it very difficult to go to the supermarket, catch public transport or travel far from home. What they fear is having a panic attack in a situation where help or escape might be difficult. Many will not venture out into unknown territory alone. Similarly, with social phobia, a person tends to avoid social situations because they find mixing with people extremely uncomfortable: they fear what the other people might think about them. No doubt disorders such as these can restrict a couple's social life, and are often a bone of contention.

Death

Eventually you will experience the death of someone close to you. Depending on who died, your relationship with your partner will be affected to varying degrees. Listening to your partner about how they feel and giving practical support in those early days is what is needed. Be aware that your expectations of their 'return to normal' may be unrealistic. Remember, when they are trying to come to terms with the death of someone close to them, there will be little emotional energy to put into your relationship. Withdrawing from you emotionally is transient and, in time, your relationship will move to a new phase.

The death of a child will have the greatest impact on the parental relationship. People grieve in their own ways, but when both people are similarly affected by the death, often difficulties that previously existed between the two are exacerbated. Seeking appropriate help is strongly recommended.

> *My mother died suddenly when I had been married for one year. My world came tumbling down. Nothing could have prepared me for my life without her. Looking back now ten years on, what surprised me was the effect her death had on my relationship. I had always been seen as someone who managed things extremely well. But when I was grieving I was not available to worry about everyone else in my life. It was enough for me to look after myself. No-one really said so, but it was as if I was expected to be back to my normal self a few months later. It was a hard time.*
>
> Karen, 34 years

As we have said before, stressful life events can alter the course of your relationship path. If the issues are not addressed, you may end up questioning your relationship, especially if you feel that your partner neglects you or doesn't listen to you. You are then vulnerable to having an affair if the situation does not right itself. In the next chapter we will look more closely at affairs and their effects.

IN BRIEF...

@ Life throws up many challenges – for example, having children, illness, work crises, family problems and death.

@ Your relationship's success is partly determined by you and your partner's ability to accommodate change.

@ See yourself as a team, and work out ways to deal with the issue you are facing.

The lighter side.....

When you first met your partner, did you act in a way to make yourself seem more attractive to them?

I went around to his house in my basketball uniform. I knew he was the sporty type and I couldn't catch a ball to save my life, but I thought it would impress him.

Tanya, 34 years

Very early on in our relationship, I stupidly invited her for dinner even though I couldn't cook. I got my sister to cook the meal and then pretended that I had done it. She didn't find out for months.

Daniel, 33 years

I pretended I was organised, tidy and fit.

Nance, 33 years

I quickly went out and bought the type of records she liked. When she went through my collection, I know she was pleased to see that we had the same taste. The funny thing was, I did begin to like all her

music, so she never knew the difference.

Mark, 42 years

For the first two weeks, I pretended I was a vegetarian because I had heard that he was. It was a great relief to find out that he wasn't. Although it did take some explaining when I began to eat red meat.

Cathy, 37 years

I never used to like sport, but because he was so into it, I quickly went and had some tennis and golf lessons. The tennis was hopeless, but I showed some potential at golf. I still haven't confessed this to him, ten years later!

Rebecca, 35 years

She swears I pretended to be rich. I don't remember it like that. I did take her out a lot and always paid, but that's how I was brought up. I never told her what I earned, but I didn't think it was necessary.

Steve, 44 years

11 CHAPTER

Surviving
an affair

Infidelity – it's a word that conjures up a range of difficult emotions. Most of you probably know someone who has either had an affair, or whose partner has had an affair. Unless you have actually been in the situation, you will not know how it feels. But we know from our work with people who have experienced the effects of affairs that what they go through is very similar to coping with any trauma. In this chapter, we'll look at the effects of affairs, ways to prevent them, and how to move on afterwards.

The effects of an affair

We define an affair as *any significant relationship that takes you away physically and/or emotionally from your committed relationship. It can include anything from a one night stand, to a regular meeting with kissing only, to a full on sexual relationship.* We strongly warn people not to kid themselves into thinking that just because they are not having sex, they are not having an affair.

At the heart of any affair is deceit. Deception is the inevitable consequence of an affair, and it can be about time, thoughts about

> **You are not committed to your partner if you are entertaining ideas about another person. You are setting yourself up for an affair.**

someone else, money, sex and where you have been. What affairs do is break the bond of commitment. You are not committed to your partner if you are entertaining ideas about another person. Of course, it's normal to find other people attractive from time to time, but actually thinking about a potential relationship with someone is dangerous.

Are you setting yourself up for an affair?

- Have you ever entertained any thoughts about another person when you have been in a relationship with someone else?
- Did you ever act on these thoughts?
- What issues were you and your partner facing at the time?

The effects on you of hearing that your partner has been having an affair will no doubt depend on your personality and experience. When the news of an affair is recent, possible feelings include:

- shock – disbelief at what has happened
- anger – feelings of injustice and senselessness; angry outbursts; 'why me?'
- numbness – feelings of detachment; feeling isolated from others
- sadness – feelings of loss; feeling alone

You might also play over in your mind the way in which you found out the news, or avoid any situations that remind you of the affair. Gradually you will begin to remember certain events that at the time did not add up. You might try to clarify these incidents with your partner, who might or might not be willing to rub salt into the wound. You are also likely to experience heightened anxiety; physical changes, such as nausea, loss of appetite and diarrhoea; and changes in your behaviour, such as withdrawing socially.

These changes, although distressing at the time, are normal and expected reactions to the news that your partner has been having an affair.

Unfortunately, what happens in many cases, after one partner discloses the news of an affair, is that they then don't want to hear anything more about it. They believe they have done their bit (disclosing the affair), and probably felt lousy and guilty in the process. They now want things to return to 'normal'. What they forget is that the relationship they once knew is now changed. It can never be retrieved.

How to rebuild after an affair

An affair doesn't have to mean the end of the relationship. Some people are able to move on together. An affair can be the catalyst for both individuals to look at their relationship. For those who do *choose* to give it another go, four things are required, once commitment is established. First, the person who had the affair needs to cease all contact with the person with whom they had the affair. Second, the person who had the affair has to be able to hear how much their partner is hurting as a result of their behaviour. Third, the person on the receiving end will need a period of time to grieve. That means grieving the loss of the relationship as they knew it. Finally, once the grieving period is over, they need to be able to assure themselves that in their mind the 'affair' is finished, and that they will not rehash it whenever the relationship hits a rough patch. That is their responsibility.

Important steps in rebuilding
To rebuild their relationship after an affair, each person needs to do the following:
The one who has had the affair:
- Cease all contact with the other person.
- Listen to your partner.

- Answer questions openly and honestly; keeping other facts hidden prevents you from beginning again with a clean slate.
- Work out where you went wrong.
- What limits do you need to set in place to keep your own behaviour in check in the future?

The one who was on the receiving end:

- Expect to feel numb for some time during the grieving process.
- Make an informed choice about whether or not you want to pursue the relationship.
- If you do want to pursue the relationship, challenge unhelpful thoughts that keep you 'stuck' and rehashing the affair.
- Set a limit for when you will stop asking questions.
- Build your own interests.
- Decide on what behaviour you will and won't tolerate.
- Counselling often helps, either individually or as a couple.

How to build trust again

There is no magical cure to rebuilding a sense of trust in a relationship once it has been abused. It takes time, patience and lots of realistic thinking. With a lack of trust comes a lowering of one's self-esteem, anxiety that it might happen again, and jealousy.

Consider James, who came for help after he learnt that his wife was having an affair. His unhelpful thinking went something like this:

> I don't want the relationship to be over, but I don't know how I will ever be able to feel totally at ease when she's out of my sight.

He challenged his thinking to include:

I have chosen to continue in our relationship. We have both decided it is where we want to be. She is sorry and wishes she could turn back time. I have to let her keep on with her own life. No amount of worry on my part will alter what she will or won't do. We had issues before that we ignored. Now we are willing to discuss these. She says she wants to be here. I have to believe her, otherwise we have nothing.

Skills for rebuilding trust

1. time to grieve
2. special time together
3. clear thinking
4. common goals
5. learning to change your behaviour for the good of your relationship

To tell or not to tell?

If you are having an affair and your partner does not know, whether you tell them or not is up to you. Each situation will be different. We suggest that you make an informed decision using our 'Framework for making choices' described in Chapter 9. Individual counselling could help you make the decision to either leave the marriage, or end the affair and build a new relationship with your partner.

Whether you attend counselling or not, two important questions that you need to answer are:

1. Is the affair finished?
2. Are you going to commit to your relationship?

If you answered 'no' to the questions above, then you have some serious thinking to do. Remaining in a relationship if you have no intention of giving it your full attention is selfish. Remaining in an affair is also selfish. You can't have your cake and eat it too. There is no commitment to either relationship.

Creating a new challenge – sparks, fulfilment and fun

If a relationship is going to survive an affair, both parties must be prepared to accept that they each have to take on the responsibility for developing a different relationship. Let's look at Andy and Marion's story.

Andy and Marion's story

Marion sought help for the distress she was feeling at the imminent departure of her husband of eighteen years. Andy had met someone else and had been open about the fact. He was delaying leaving the family home for practical reasons, and because Marion had asked him to stay. Both fronted up for counselling on day one – Marion to see what she could do to stop him leaving, and Andy to see if he could get a professional blessing for the decision he had made. Much to their surprise, counselling focused on their relationship. The reasons for their initial attraction and the longevity of the marriage were all discussed at length. To Marion's horror, the problems in their marriage were tackled next. Andy was full of reasons why the marriage had not been perfect. ***There are no sparks left. It is not fulfilling anymore. We don't have any fun.*** In his new woman, Andy believed he would find these things: sparks, fulfilment and fun.

When we began to work on how sparks, fulfilment and fun could be refactored into the marriage, an interesting thing happened. Andy began to lose courage about pursuing the new woman. He began to notice slight imperfections. He still believed she was the one he should choose, but he began to have his doubts. Marion remained tremendously strong. She continued to find ways to look after herself. She continued to discuss ways to improve the marriage. She remained patient. Her reactions surprised Andy. He had been expecting to be thrown out. He had hoped he would be thrown out! It would have made his decision easier. Marion was determined not to make it easy for him to go, but rather to accept the challenge to improve their marriage, which had not been cared for over the years.

Now, six months later, Andy still thinks of the other woman. But he thinks of her as being in the past. He is relieved he didn't throw away his marriage. Marion still thinks of her too – she hopes she is in the past and looks forward to her future with Andy.

For any relationship to move forward after an affair, it is therefore essential that a new challenge or focus is created. How you go about achieving this goal is perhaps easier to contemplate if you accept that the person who has been unfaithful can again leave at any time, regardless of what you do or don't do. It's up to them. You can only do what you believe is right for you. There are no guarantees, not even in the best of relationships. At the end of the day, all you can do is cross your fingers.

> **It is possible to rebuild your relationship after an affair if commitment is established.**

The positive domino effect

Remember we outlined the positive domino effect in Chapter 8? Let's look at how we can apply this principle to create a new challenge after one partner has had an affair.

You both need to ask yourself: *What can I do differently to effect a positive change?* The aim is to create a positive domino effect where your behaviour sparks a positive reaction. To do this effectively involves identifying what things in your relationship *you* can do differently to create this positive effect. It might mean actively doing something differently, or letting go of something else.

For a relationship to survive an affair, both parties have to choose to give the relationship another go. It is therefore a joint responsibility to do things differently and, as such, create a new relationship.

> *I know I had grown to rely on him too much. I wasn't as independent as I had been before and this irritated him. My dependency didn't cause the affair, but it probably affected how he saw me. So I developed my own interests. I now have a hectic social life and our relationship is much better for it.*
>
> Gena, 44 years

IN BRIEF...

@ Any affair breaks the bond of commitment.

@ It is possible to rebuild after an affair if commitment is established.

The lighter side......

Why?

- Why do men blow their nose in the shower?
- Why do some men sweep their hair over their bald spot?
- Why do men have an obsession with the remote control?
- Why do men waste their time reading the television guide throughout the program they chose to watch?
- Why do men always want a cuddle whenever women are using a sharp knife?

- Why are grown men still obsessed with their bowels?
- Why do men always remember what they need to do for work, but never at home?
- Why do women get a cold and men get the flu?
- Why do men need to read on the toilet?
- Why do men need to read on the toilet for such a long time?
- Why do men always think of the negative side of an idea before they think of the positives?

CHAPTER 12

Think before you cyber

A young woman telephones the radio station and requests a song for the 'man she lives for' – a man from Egypt whom she has never met, let alone seen. However, the young woman on the airwaves believes her man in Egypt is 'perfect' for her and makes her life worthwhile. The DJ gently asks whether she thinks they will eventually meet. She sadly replies, 'Probably not.'

Internet relationships, while bringing many people together who would never otherwise meet, are fraught with difficulties. If you are single and meet someone on the Internet, you face potential problems such as geographical separation that make the progression of the relationship difficult. Furthermore, an Internet attachment prevents you from being 'emotionally available' to meet someone locally. In this chapter, we'll look at the effects the Internet is having on relationships.

The Internet

Unfortunately, in our practice we are hearing about more and more people whose existing relationships are being threatened by

Internet romances. Where should the line be drawn about what behaviour is acceptable and what behaviour is dangerous or unacceptable? Many people think Internet relationships are permissible because they don't cross the sexual boundary. We disagree. Any relationship or 'contact' with another person that removes you, or part of you, from the relationship with your partner is dangerous. For example, consider Tony who came for help to work out how to handle the fact that his wife was meeting men in chat rooms on the Internet.

Tony's story (48 years)

She's told me that she is not happy in our marriage. We have three beautiful children but she feels that life is passing her by. We met and married when we were both very young. Up until now, she has always been there; now I come home and she's on the Internet. She tells me that she spends most of the hours that the children are at school chatting to people on the other side of the world. I have tolerated this behaviour for months now, not wanting to rock the boat. In a way, I believed that it might help her by giving her the opportunity to meet people.

Recently, however, she has been chatting to a few specific men and she seems different. Some have expressed interest in meeting her. She tells me she talks about us and her unhappiness in our marriage. I'm now worried and jealous. It's eating me up. She's not having sex with someone else, but she may as well be. I feel totally betrayed and I'm not sure if I can keep pretending that nothing is really happening.

Tony's story is all too familiar. The problem is that what initially starts out as friendly communication can end up spinning a web of lies and deceit. Before long, the person involved in an Internet liaison is spending more and more time on-line, having more and more of their needs met by a person they don't really know. An Internet partner can be anyone they like; they can create an illusion. How do you know they are who they say they are? Even though we often think the grass is greener somewhere else, it can in fact be browner.

We believe that our society's ethical and moral guidelines have not yet caught up with technology. The rules of Internet relationships have yet to be prescribed. Our belief is that Internet relationships are no different from conventional affairs. Affairs are not just about physical sex; they are about betrayal, lies, deceit, rejection and lack of commitment. That intercourse has not yet, and may never, occur in Internet liaisons is irrelevant – there is still deceit. If you are unsure as to whether you are crossing the boundary, answer the questions in the box below.

Is your Internet relationship getting out of hand?

1. Do you long to tell your Internet partner rather than your actual partner about something exciting in your life?
2. Does the communication you share on-line take up valuable time that you could be spending with your partner, children, friends or on your own activities?
3. Do you mostly communicate with one special person on-line?
4. Are you aware of when they will be on-line?
5. Do you try to think of ways that you might be able to actually meet your Internet partner?
6. Have you ever engaged in 'cyber sex' with your Internet partner? ('Cyber sex' means communicating in a suggestive or erotic manner via the Internet while self-stimulating.)
7. Would you feel down if you were unable to correspond with your Internet partner for a period of time?

You may not have answered 'yes' to any of these questions, but if you are planning to continue the communication with someone on the Internet, keep these questions in mind as time goes by. At the end of the day, it is your reliance on that special Internet partner that can lead to difficulties in your own relationship.

Steps to bring your Internet affair to an end

If you answered 'yes' to any of the questions in 'Is your Internet relationship getting out of hand?', we suggest you:

1. Write down the answers to the above questions.
2. Stop your Internet contact immediately.
3. Consider the likely consequences for yourself, your partner and your children if you were to continue in your Internet relationship.
4. Start working on identifying any problems in your relationship that need to be addressed.
5. Reaffirm your commitment to your partner.
6. Make sure your behaviour reflects this commitment – and that means giving up the Internet liaison.

The nature of Internet relationships

There are a number of factors that distinguish Internet relationships from normal everyday relationships or friendships. These key factors include: availability of the Internet, accessibility, frequency of use and the actual amount of time spent on-line. Because Internet relationships are easy – and by that we mean little effort is needed – users soon become reliant and dependent on them. They start to fill the needs that would otherwise be met by your partner or other friends.

The Internet keeps you in the 'bubble'

Having an intimate relationship on the Internet keeps you constantly in the bubble of new love because there is no pressure from the outside world. There is just you and your belief in this perfect partner who is always available and understanding. Your Internet relationship can easily be put on hold while you deal with the rest of your life. Once you've dealt with the matter at hand, you can pick up where you left off – it remains unaffected.

Internet relationships are not deep, but they lull the participants into thinking that they are. In fact, they are superficial as there is no duty of care associated with them, no reality check. When a person starts an Internet relationship, it's as if they are in fantasy land where there are no real consequences for their behaviour.

> **Internet affairs are affairs because they reflect a lack of commitment.**

Email

The upside of the Internet in relationships is when it is used as a communication tool. And, of course, there will be a small percentage of people who develop a wonderful relationship, and then go on to have a normal everyday relationship, with someone whom they met via the Net. However, we think that these people are in the minority.

Unfortunately, there are associated problems with the use of email as a communication tool because the written word is open to misinterpretation due to the absence of verbal and nonverbal signals. Without platitudes, intonations and an immediate ability to check out what is meant, misunderstandings can easily occur.

> *We finally met in person after we'd known each other for about a year on the Internet. I really liked her but I'd have to say that it is now very different and nothing can compare to the real thing.*
>
> Chris, 23 years

When simple communication on the Internet develops into friendship or romantic interest, something as simple as: *I can't talk to my husband as easily as you* may be interpreted by another person as: *You want me and you are willing to leave your husband for me.* One big problem is that you cannot readily check out past hurts and, most importantly, the neediness of the person with whom you are communicating, because you are removed from their environment and other sources of information.

Think before you send

Another problem with the use of emails in relationships is that they are immediate. With a simple push of a button, anything you thought and felt at one time can be delivered in an instant. Even in established relationships, people get caught in the trap of having 'deep and meaningfuls' via the Net. We strongly recommend that you sleep on any difficult communication with a partner via the Net. (A similar warning applies to the writing and sending of conventional letters.) By all means type it up, but don't send it then. Leave it for at least a day, and give yourself time to check your thinking in what you have written. More importantly, ask yourself: *What are the consequences of what I have written?* Remember, emotions go up and down, and if you write and send on a day when you're feeling down, you might view your situation completely differently on a day when you believe things are going

> **Try to avoid exchanging deep and meaningful emails with your partner or Internet partner because they are open to complete misinterpretation.**

well. We would actually go so far as to advise you not to have deep and meaningful communications via the Net with anyone, because without a common context, and verbal and nonverbal cues, everything you write is open to misinterpretation. Most people would acknowledge that it's hard to have a discussion on the telephone about difficult emotional issues; well, the Internet is even harder.

> *I had an awful experience at work when I accidentally sent a very graphic love letter to the wrong person by mistake – I selected the wrong name and hit the send button before I realised. The person who received it was flattered and, before long, half the company knew. I've never been so embarrassed.*
>
> Sarah, 24 years

IN BRIEF...

@ Internet affairs are affairs.

@ Communication via the Internet is open to misinterpretation.

The lighter side......

Why?

- Why do women talk so much?
- Why do women rush around cleaning the house before the cleaners arrive?
- Why do women tell their partners not to make a fuss about their birthday or anniversary, and then sulk for days when their instruction is heeded?
- Why do women keep forgetting that men always think of the negative side of an idea before the positives?
- Why do women so easily dismiss compliments?
- Why do women suddenly start to wear old ladies' clothes when they reach a certain age?
- Why do women worry so much about what other people think?

13 | The grass is often browner

Why do affairs happen? As we have been discussing in the previous chapters, affairs can be the result of dissatisfaction in a relationship, underlying problems which have not been addressed, or a sadness that the relationship has changed with time. Another precursor to affairs is thinking that the grass is greener in someone else's yard. This way of thinking can lead to feelings of envy, resentment and discontent. We have seen the result of many people acting on this way of thinking and ending up just as, or even more, unhappy. In this chapter we would like to look at the effects of thinking that the grass is greener with someone else.

So, you are thinking of leaving

Perhaps you have met someone else, or have even begun a relationship with another person. You are probably comparing the current state of your marriage with your feelings for this new person. There is no real comparison. They are like chalk and cheese. But is this comparison true or fair, taking into account the fact that you are back in the bubble of new love, where nothing seems a problem?

Remember our earlier discussion on the bubble of new love? In the bubble, the relationship is out of step with the real world as it has not yet been affected by the ups and downs of day-to-day life. In this intact form, it is very appealing. But, is your perception of this new relationship real? If there is a chance that the bubble is blocking out the effects of the rest of your life, then this is not a stable basis on which to make a very important decision. We warn people against making a decision based on a feeling, because feelings change.

Since you cannot compare the current state of your marriage with the new, bubble-affected relationship, it can be of some use to compare the embryonic stages of your relationship with your partner with your new relationship. While this can still be dangerous, since it is easy to forget past pleasures and pain, it is a good place to start. Try to think back to those early days. What first attracted you to your partner? What were the best parts about falling in love? How was the sex? What did it feel like to be in the bubble with your partner? How often did you argue? What behaviours were you more tolerant about in those early days? The answers to these questions can help to put both relationships in perspective. You just cannot compare chalk and cheese.

The cost of divorce

When you are busy comparing 'chalk' and 'cheese' in the way described above, it is easy to be blind to the costs of divorce. The costs are both emotional and financial, and affect your partner, your children and, definitely, you.

These costs need to be taken into consideration when deciding whether or not to leave a marriage. It is also important that you examine the nature of the problems in your current relationship. Answering the following questions may help.

A checklist of common relationship difficulties

1. Are our family histories very different?
2. Have we any interests in common?
3. Do we have enough individual interests?
4. Are our life priorities different?
5. Do we have similar values?
6. Do we have individual and common goals?
7. Are we reacting to each other's personality?
8. Do our parenting styles vary considerably?
9. Are we having sexual difficulties?
10. Am I feeling misunderstood?

After answering each of these questions, ask yourself: *Was this always the case?* If 'yes', then the prognosis is poorer than if the answer is 'no'.

If the difficulties have not always been there, then using the problem-solving strategies in this book, or attending counselling, may help to address the issues that are interfering with your contentment. After addressing some of these issues, you might be able to make a more informed decision about whether to leave your relationship.

Using the framework for making choices

When people are faced with a difficult decision, such as whether to leave a relationship or not, the same questions come up: *How do I choose? How will I know if I am making the right decision?* Our standard framework for making choices is helpful if you are considering leaving your current relationship.

Below is an example of how the framework can be used. Jason had met somebody else and was contemplating leaving his wife to pursue a relationship with this woman. He was encouraged to use the framework in an attempt to make this most difficult decision. Jason's answers to the relevant questions illustrate how the framework is used.

Framework for making choices

Jason, 44 years

1. What is the problem you are experiencing? (Be specific.)

   I have been getting closer to a female colleague and, although we have not had an affair, I'm thinking of leaving my wife and starting a relationship with my colleague.

2. How many possible solutions can you suggest for this problem? (Don't worry about how ridiculous they might seem.)

   (a) *I could leave straightaway and start the new relationship.*

   (b) *I could leave straightaway and be on my own for a while.*

   (c) *I could stay with my wife and not confront the problems we have been having.*

   (d) *I could stay with my wife and attempt to address some of our problems.*

3. What are the positives and negatives of each of these possible solutions?

   (a) Pos: *Wouldn't have to think anymore – just act!*

       Neg: *Seems a bit drastic. Not giving marriage a chance. What if new relationship doesn't work?*

   (b) Pos: *May give me a chance to see things clearly from a distance.*

       Neg: *I would be lonely and I might miss out on a relationship with either.*

   (c) Pos: *I wouldn't feel guilty. Fewer financial problems.*

       Neg: *We would continue to fight and end up resenting each other even more.*

   (d) Pos: *At least I would feel good about attempting to resolve the issues we have. Who knows, we may even work things out. Fewer financial problems. Better for the children if it does work out.*

> *Neg: I may miss the opportunity of a relationship with my colleague.*

4. Which looks best to you? (Which has the most positives?)
   d) Attempting to resolve things with my wife.

5. If you used this solution, what would the consequences be?
   I probably would lose the opportunity with the other woman. We may not be able to work together anymore.

6. What steps do you need to take to try this solution out?
   Talk to my wife about getting some counselling. Putting a priority on time together to address problems. Not spending any time alone with colleague.

7. Once you have done it, are you happy with the outcome?
   We are seeing a couple counsellor. It's hard work because it's bringing up a lot of issues. Sometimes I wonder if it would have been easier to have just walked.

8. If you are not happy with your choice, are there any little changes that would improve the outcome? If not, go back to step 2 and rework the steps.
   I might suggest we do something fun together every now and then – not just concentrate on the negatives.

Because Jason was encouraged to think rationally and objectively, he was able to make an informed choice. There is far less chance of regret this way than if he had made a random or impulsive decision.

We see many people, like Jason, who entertain the idea of leaving their partner for somebody else. We also see many people who wish they could leave, but don't for a number of reasons. If you find yourself thinking a lot about somebody else, then we suggest that you need to take some drastic action. If you have no intention of leaving your relationship, then you are only setting yourself up to slip off your relationship path.

THE GRASS IS OFTEN BROWNER | 169

If you find yourself in such a predicament, we recommend the following ground rules:

Ground rules for preventing the development of an affair

1. Remove yourself from any situation that places your relationship in jeopardy.
2. List the damage that is likely if this infatuation escalates.
3. Challenge your unhelpful thinking.
4. Resist the urge to compare your relationship with this new love or infatuation. You can't compare chalk and cheese.
5. Start with your behaviour: with your partner set up some positive couple time, which doesn't involve deep and meaningful conversations. Strive to have some fun together.
6. Rethink what your commitment means to you and ask yourself the following: *Am I willing to give this up? What are the consequences of giving up my relationship?*
7. Put yourself in your partner's shoes for a moment. How would you cope if they were contemplating beginning a new relationship and you hadn't been given the chance to fight for what you wanted?

And what if things just feel stale?

All long-term relationships fall into a rut from time to time. During such phases, you may become very vulnerable to having an affair. Many people tell us that they happened to meet someone for whom they just fell and therefore had to leave their marriage. The truth probably was that their marriage had been in a rut and they had not addressed their problems, and then gave in to the temptation of being with someone new and exciting.

> **A stale marriage is no reason to leave.**

It takes a constant effort to keep the spark alive in a marriage. But as we have been discussing, the grass is often browner with someone else, and so the answer is not necessarily to find someone else. Instead, if your relationship is feeling stale, take the preventative step of exploring potential areas of difficulty. Remember the questions we listed at the beginning of this chapter ('A checklist of common relationship difficulties' on p. 166)? It is useful to answer these questions in the context of a stale marriage.

By answering these questions you may realise that you are both working towards very different goals, or that you are not having enough time on your own, or that you are battling with each other over parenting. If you are having problems in any of the areas listed earlier, they can all be addressed. Just because there are issues doesn't mean that it's the beginning of the end. Because all marriages have these down times, the strategies we discuss in this book are worth following in an attempt to minimise the lows and maximise the highs.

Have a look at our list of ways to revamp a stale relationship and then adopt any strategy which appeals to both of you.

Ways to revamp a stale relationship

- Attend a regular activity together as a couple.
- Have a night out alone on a regular basis.
- Have a night away together whenever you can.
- Change predictable routines, especially those concerning your sex life and social activities.
- Do something you used to enjoy doing years before.
- Go somewhere you used to go years before.
- Have a good laugh over something.
- Dance.
- Develop some common goals for one, five and ten years down the track.

> *Whenever I think our relationship needs a boost, I book our favourite cheap restaurant. It's where we spent many nights before we were married. It means a bit of a drive and some organisation, but we usually end up reminiscing and enjoying ourselves.*
>
> Judy, 38 years

Don't stand in the way of temptation

When the relationship is feeling a bit stale, it can be very tempting to seek the company of new people. You might believe that you could never stray. You might simply think that you are enjoying someone else's company. You probably are not even considering your marriage when you have that lunch or drink with that colleague or friend. The truth is, however, that if you find this person at all attractive, or if that person makes it known that they are attracted to you, keep away! Things can move from innocent get togethers to infidelity pretty quickly. By keeping out of the way of temptation, you will not have to rely on willpower to resist the charms of someone with whom you have been spending a lot of time alone.

The midlife crisis

A well known precursor to thinking that the grass would be greener with someone else is the midlife crisis. In our opinion it is mostly a male phenomenon. Some midlife crises occur at 30, some at 40, and some at 50 years of age. It's therefore not the age per se that triggers a midlife crisis, but how you are thinking about what is happening in your life at the time. It might be the questioning of a career path, dissatisfaction with your relationship, or concern about your health. What tends to happen, however, is that your relationship takes the full impact of your self-doubt. The self-doubt *is* actually the midlife crisis.

At that point, the self-doubt takes on a life of its own. What then happens can be dangerous. You might begin to question your

> **Midlife crises are about self-doubt. What is it within yourself that you need to change?**

relationship and your feelings for your partner. If you begin to reminisce about life in the bubble and how good you felt then, you mistakingly look for ways to recapture that feeling of new love. This can have dire consequences, especially if you begin to look for a new partner.

Some signs that someone may be heading for a midlife crisis

- questioning what they have achieved, their lifestyle, and so on
- irritability
- withdrawal from partner
- increased criticism of partner
- buying a car which is very different to their usual style
- trendy new clothes and glasses
- modern haircut unlike any other they have had
- socialising with younger crowd at work

Peter's story (52 years)

Peter looked as if he'd been through the wringer. He sat wiping back the tears as he told of his pain. He was 52 years old, married with two children. He had a good job, but one he found particularly stressful. He said that for a long time he hadn't felt happy either personally or professionally.

I began working with Jane, a colleague, on a new project two years ago. Gradually, we started spending more and more time together, which I could easily hide from my family under the guise of working back late at the office. I thought a lot about her and wanted to be with her. I bought a new car to impress her. Thinking about having an affair shocked me greatly, but it didn't stop me pursuing her. I had felt bored at home for a long time. I love my wife but not in the same way. Before long, Jane and I were together; it was so intense. I felt something that I haven't felt before. The sex was great; it was never like that with my wife. We kept on with the affair for eighteen months without my wife's knowledge. A few weeks ago, I blurted it out because I could no longer keep the secret and I wanted out of my marriage. But now, I've stuffed Jane around for so long that she has told me not to contact her unless I'm going to leave my marriage. I just don't know what to do. Last week I thought I needed to stay for the kids and try and make my marriage work. Now I'm not so sure. I don't know if I can do it.

Typical of someone suffering from a 'midlife' crisis, Peter was full of self-doubt. In therapy it was discovered that there was a certain level of instability in the company where he worked. Colleagues – whom he had believed to be as worthwhile, if not more so, than him – had been retrenched. He had voiced his concern to his wife, but she had not seemed all that interested.

Jane, on the other hand, thought he was wonderful. She believed in his abilities and told him this often. When he expressed concern over his job security to her, she came up with 100 reasons why the company would never let him go and, if they did, she assured him that he would find another job in a flash.

It also became evident that Peter was unhappy with the frequency of sex with his wife, and the decreasing amount of spontaneity and adventure. His suggestions were dismissed by his wife, which had the effect of creating self-doubt about his attractiveness to women. Jane definitely showed him otherwise.

The goal of therapy was to first help Peter become aware of these areas of self-doubt. Second, he was helped to examine his options based on this greater insight into himself. Third, if Peter decides to give his marriage another try, he and his wife would benefit from couple counselling by looking at the way in which they communicate. Peter had tried on several occasions to voice his concerns to his wife. She had seemed uninterested. Why? There could be many reasons, including built-up resentment, feeling neglected and not knowing *how* to listen. Regardless of these, the responsibility lay with Peter to be the first to speak, since it was he who was feeling dissatisfied.

For those who can never commit

There are a group of men and women who cannot commit to a relationship because they are always wondering – *What if the grass is greener with someone else? What if there is someone more suitable for me? What if we are just not right for each other?* When we hear people asking these questions, without any real foundation, we start to wonder about their ability to commit to anyone. In order to test this theory, we explore difficulties in their current relationship and the helpfulness of their thinking. If there do not appear to be any real issues, and their thinking is solely focused on the idea of there being someone better out there for them, we would set about examining the idea of commitment. As you will remember, commitment is the key to any successful relationship.

IN BRIEF...

@ The grass is not always greener with someone else.
@ You cannot compare the current state of your marriage with feelings you might have for a new person.
@ You need to be fully aware of the difficulties in your relationship.
@ Try to make informed decisions about your relationship.
@ There are many ways to revamp a stale relationship.

The lighter side......

Here's another little gem from the Internet (source unknown).

Why nagging a man doesn't work

What a woman says:
'This place is a mess! C'mon,
you and I need to clean up,
your stuff is lying on the floor
and you'll have no clothes to wear,
if we don't do the washing right now!'

What a man hears:
'Blah, blah, blah, blah, C'MON,
Blah, blah, blah, blah, YOU AND I,
Blah, blah, blah, blah, ON THE FLOOR,
Blah, blah, blah, blah, NO CLOTHES,
Blah, blah, blah, blah, RIGHT NOW!'

It it's over – what now?

No matter how hard you might work at rebuilding your relationship after an affair, or at revamping a stale relationship, the reality is that some relationships do break up. Perhaps you instigated the break-up or perhaps it was forced upon you. Whatever the reason, it is now up to you to move on. The emotions you experience when a relationship ends, especially if you are on the receiving end, are very much like those experienced by people who are grieving. The intensity of the emotion might not be quite as strong, but the reality is that it hurts as though the person has, in fact, died. In a sense, that person has died for you. They are no longer who they were to you. Some people in this situation say it would be easier for them if their partner had died, rather than having made the deliberate choice to leave them.

In this chapter, we look at what you need to do to move on after a relationship has ended. We examine why relationships fail, ways to make a clean break from your ex-partner, and how to go about choosing a new partner when the time is right.

How to move on

You can't successfully move on until the past is resolved. Making sense of what went wrong is an important step in moving forward. No-one deliberately repeats old mistakes but, unfortunately, it happens. Dan came to counselling after he found that he was preparing to leave his second marriage.

Dan's story (49 years)

I can't believe I am having counselling. Nine years ago I never would have believed that I would be here talking about leaving my second wife. We were so happy. I met her just after I had left my first wife. My first marriage had been a disaster from day one. When I left, I assumed that we were not compatible, and that she was just too complicated for me. Unfortunately, I had to leave behind two teenage children. I only see one of them now.

I met my current wife at a work do and we seemed to click straightaway. I felt relieved that I was not going to be on my own after all, and we saw each other pretty much every day. My kids weren't very happy at first, but they got used to the idea of me having someone new, and we married after nine months.

We were really happy for the first five years, moderately happy for the next two, and have been terribly unhappy for the last two. Things did get harder after we had our daughter, but I expected us to get back to normal. Our relationship has not recovered. Our sex life just dropped off after our daughter was born – just like in my first marriage. I was patient and understanding for six months or so, but then became resentful. After a while, I just gave up trying. She is so preoccupied with our daughter, she doesn't give me much attention at all. The same thing happened after my first wife had our children. I've come to the conclusion that there is just a big conspiracy out there among women. They just want to have babies and then they give up. I think I'll just give up too.

It's easy to see how hurt Dan is. He had no real idea about what went wrong in his first marriage and had assumed that the new relationship would work. He is just as ignorant about what is going on in his current relationship. Nothing is being addressed and so nothing will be resolved. He certainly learnt that the grass is often just as brown with someone else. Counselling is helping Dan to look at how he likes to pretend problems aren't there, how personally he takes a sexual rejection, and how unrealistic his expectations about relationships and children are.

Why is there such a high rate of failure in second marriages? There can be many reasons. These include the fact that often people are attracted to similar types of people. The match between you and someone with a certain personality may not be made in heaven. Also, you might not have been aware of the problems that caused the breakdown of your first marriage which therefore makes it hard to prevent them from developing again. There might be difficulties with step-families and ex-partners. You might have left your marriage for the wrong reasons and regret the decision. Finally, your partner might leave you.

Why did it fail?

There will never be one single reason why any relationship fails. What tends to happen is that over time people behave in certain ways and the relationship ends up getting stuck in the same rut. People become more intolerant of each other's differences, and then focus more on the negatives. This leads to a gradual erosion of the good things. The reasons why they were first attracted to each other get lost in the process. You may be able to identify with some of the typical pitfalls in relationships we describe below.

The doormat – being too self-sacrificing

Becoming a doormat is a gradual process. The type of personality that lends itself to being a doormat would be seen as being very positive in a relationship at first. This person may have been caring, 'easy-going' to the point of being somewhat passive, and having a tendency to put the needs of their partner ahead of their own. What happens over time is that this person can develop into being too self-sacrificing. By that we mean allowing themselves to be walked over so that their own needs are ignored to their detriment. The person who is doing the walking over can eventually tire of having a partner who doesn't stand up for themselves.

The ostrich – avoids major issues

The ostrich does what an ostrich does best; buries its head in the sand. They are the avoiders of important issues. What happens is that the problems are not discussed openly; often they are swept under the carpet. In time, the pile under the carpet becomes so big that it can no longer be ignored. It is often too late then for the relationship to be salvaged as resentment has festered.

> *I did everything for him. It took ages for the penny to drop that I hadn't helped our relationship by neglecting my own needs.*
>
> Cathy, 44 years

> *No matter how many times I begged him, he would never discuss the things that made me so unhappy. In the end, I just had to go. We've now been apart two years.*
>
> Sarah, 36 years

The power struggle – both want control

Constant power struggles are tiring. Both partners tend to be competitive and like to be in control. Initially, power struggles might be seen as healthy and challenging in a relationship, especially if the balance of power swings fairly evenly between the two. When important issues such as parenting arise, a united front needs to be presented. Further, constantly debating issues wears people down, and can often lead to an increased focus on the negatives in a relationship.

The grass is greener – lack of commitment

As we wrote in Chapter 13, 'the grass is greener' refers to thinking that things are better elsewhere. Thinking this way means that you are setting yourself up to slide down the slippery slope to a lack of commitment. Giving your relationship a low priority or having an affair are two possible consequences of believing that the grass may be greener with someone else.

Separate paths – no common goals

Relationships need nurturing to survive. As we said in the beginning, all relationships follow a path. While we say that everyone

> *We just grew apart. We were both busy with our own careers. Before we even realised, we were spending less and less time together. We had different friends and different interests.*
>
> Jane, 34 years

needs individual goals, being in a relationship means having common goals as well. If you and your partner fail to keep sight of each other and do not maintain common goals and interests, then you can quite easily find yourselves on different paths.

Parenting your partner

Relationships can break down when one person falls into the habit of being more of a parent to their partner than an equal. A woman may 'mother' her partner by fussing over him and doing everything for him. Such behaviours may work well in a mother–child relationship, but they are not appropriate between two adults. Similarly, a man may 'father' his partner by being overly protective. In both cases, the sexual relationship may be most affected because no-one wants to have sex with their parent.

The split team – competition

The splitting of the team can occur for many reasons. The underlying problem is that when a couple is faced with an issue, they end up point scoring and seeing each other as the enemy instead of attempting to deal with it as a team. We see this when couples come face to face with stressful life events such as having a baby, work problems and other personal crises. One or both partners don't feel supported, which leads to resentment, anger and hurt.

Cracked foundation – major differences

The cracked foundation refers to fundamental differences between a couple that were always there, but ignored. It usually takes a while for the full extent of the crack to become obvious, probably because in the early days the positives outweighed the negatives. In time, the differences can no longer be ignored. These might include different expectations and different morals and values.

Life changes

When it comes to relationships, experiencing major life events can sometimes be the straw that breaks the camel's back. The issues have probably always been there but it is not until a significant life event – such as the death of a child, financial hardship or chronic illness – that the old issues come to the fore. Usually both partners react differently to the event, and one or both believe that they have not been understood. This belief, in turn, develops into resentment and further pain. It is not uncommon to see relationships break down after tragedy at some point down the track.

If your relationship has recently broken up, either by choice or otherwise, it is a useful exercise to try to identify into which pit you might have fallen. This is the only way that you will maximise the chance that you won't let history repeat itself.

Try not to become a victim

Work hard not to fall into the victim role if your partner has left you. We know, easier said than done. Some people, who have been left, relish their roles as victims; others are not aware that they have become one. But we are suggesting that in order to move on with your life, you need to accept that life without someone who doesn't love you, or is not committed to you, is better than life with that person.

It is also worthwhile to note that remaining in victim mode can lead to a greater chance of depression, since the term 'victim' implies a lack of control. True, you may not have any control over the fact that your partner decided to end the relationship. But you do have control over what you learn from your partner's behaviour and your own during the relationship. You do have control over how much you develop new interests and new friendships. You do have control over whether you want to have anything to do with your ex-partner.

If you find it hard to let go of what happened, it may help to ask yourself: *How does it help me to keep blaming him/her?* If you do keep rehashing what was done to you, the consequences are that you'll remain 'stuck' and become bitter and cynical. In the end, this will prevent you from developing a new relationship with someone else.

When you should end it

There are times when, despite how hard it may seem, **you** need to walk away from a relationship. By staying with someone who is not committed to you, you are putting your self-esteem at risk. Two clear examples are being involved with someone who has a commitment phobia or someone who wants to have their cake and eat it too.

Commitment phobia

'Commitment phobia' is a term that's thrown around a lot these days. Men and women are often being accused of having this **disorder** when they have a string of relationships which do not lead to marriage or the purchasing of property. So what are the signs of commitment phobia?

Signs of commitment phobia
The person who has a commitment phobia often displays some of the following behaviours:

- Often very intense at first, very passionate.
- Talks of the future soon after first start dating.
- Often extravagant with gifts.
- After a while, fobs off questions about the future.
- Will not plan holidays too far in advance.
- Talks of individual pursuits only.
- Starts to find more faults in partner.
- Postpones wedding date or moving in together.
- Can sabotage the relationship by having an affair.

These are the signs of commitment phobia, but what is the cause of it? Psychologically speaking, commitment phobia is usually caused by a fear of abandonment. Put simply, because a person is so afraid of being hurt or left by someone they love, they keep that person at arm's length to protect themselves. Sabotaging things which mean a lot to you is a common form of defense. It allows the fearful person to feel in control of the situation. That is, if they are responsible for the breakdown in the relationship, they cope better than if they really tried hard and the other person abandoned them. Looking at Nick's story helps to illustrate the components of fear of commitment more easily.

Nick's story (30 years)

I was 22 when I first started dating. I had three relationships, each lasting about 18 months before I met Alison. I was smitten from the start.

She was great and I wanted to spend every moment with her. If she had married me that first week we met, I would have been over the moon. We moved in together three months later, after I had begged and begged her. I really thought this was it.

After we had been living together for two years, Alison got restless. She started talking about marriage and having a baby. I was uncomfortable at first, and didn't really discuss it. The more she talked about the future, the more unhappy I got. I started working later and arranging more nights out with my friends. I talked of needing more space. I told her I was not sure when I would be able to have a holiday. Alison nagged me more. She annoyed me more and more. I moved out suddenly, without warning.

I only went to counselling because all my friends said I was mad for giving up Alison. They were all married and having children and I was on my own pretending to be happy about it. I dated other women, but no-one measured up to Alison.

In counselling I talked about my mother leaving my father. They had both told me it was mutual, but my fourteen-year-old mind saw things differently. I saw dad taking years to get over her, remarrying twice, and remaining bitter. When I met Alison, I honestly thought I had met the person I would be with for the rest of my life. Now I know I was right, but my fear of ending up like my father was constantly there. The closer we became, the more I felt like running. I guess it's too late now.

Nick's story is terribly sad – for both him and Alison. There is hope for him, however. When he came for counselling, he learnt a lot about challenging his unhelpful thoughts. His diary looked like this:

A - - - - **B** ~~~~ **C** .... **D** ~~~~ **E**

Situation	Thoughts	Feelings/Behaviour	New thoughts	New feelings/Behaviour
Alison talks about getting married.	*I really love her. What if she leaves me? I won't be able to live without her.*	Scared/Don't discuss future. Test her love by withdrawing mine.	*Alison is Alison. She's not my mum. She's worth the risk. I need to stop running, otherwise I'll lose what I really want.*	Still scared/Be honest. Stop testing.

You can see from Nick's diary that he talked about *testing* Alison's love for him. People who have trouble committing often do this. They think that by making it really difficult for their partner, they must be loved very much if the other person is willing to put up with this treatment. Of course, a lot of this thinking and this behaviour is going on without insight. That is, the commitment phobic often has no idea why they act the way they do. Counselling really helped Nick come to terms with his fear of abandonment. He was then able to consider taking the risk of being hurt. Time will tell if it is too late for him and Alison. We recommended that they have some couple counselling to increase the chance of a happy future together, if that's what they both wanted.

It needs to be said that because the term 'commitment phobic' has become so clichéd, we frequently counsel couples where one person accuses the other of having the problem. It is often the case that the other person has legitimate reasons for not wanting to commit. Trying to convince a person they have a fear of commitment, and therefore of abandonment, when they simply do not want a future with their partner, is pointless. Counselling can then become a forum in which a decision is made to commit or end the relationship.

The cake eaters

There are many people who do not want to commit to a relationship, not because they are **scared** of committing, but because they want to have their cake and eat it too. By committing to one person, they would have to give up other people they might be seeing. They would have to stop looking for greener grass. In a nutshell, there would be a sacrifice. It can be hard for the person who is in love with the cake eater to recognise the need to end the relationship because the cake eater throws enough crumbs to keep them interested.

> I thought he loved me. We were so good together. He never talked about the future, but he rang me every day. He would be furious if I couldn't see him when he was available. I was shocked to learn that he never had any intention of marrying me.
>
> Ruth, 31 years

To gauge whether your partner is a cake eater, you need to first look for the signs of not being committed we have listed. Second, you need to be aware of what happens when *you* withdraw slightly. Although we don't encourage anybody to play games, it can be interesting to see what happens when you hold back from a person who is showing signs of not being committed. If they want their cake and want to eat it too, they will make much more of an effort when you hold back. As soon as you are attentive again, they will decrease their effort.

This phenomenon is most likely to become obvious in your sexual relationship. As long as you keep having sex with the person who is showing signs of not being committed, they are going to be having it all. What do you think would happen if you stopped having sex with them? Either the

> I told her she was the one I wanted to stay with. I thought she wanted me too. It turns out she did want me, but she wanted a lot of others too. She said she was only sleeping with me, but wanted the freedom to see other people.
>
> Glen, 38 years

> As soon as I said
> 'no' to sex, he no
> longer called. I later
> heard that he began
> seeing someone
> else two days later.
>
> Susie, 27 years

individual will try harder to get everything they want, but still not commit, or they will give up on you and move on quite quickly. Either option shows them up for what they were – not serious about the relationship. You then need to ask yourself: *Is this the type of relationship in which I want to be?*

Remember, if you want to be in a committed relationship, you **both** need to be committed to it, not just you. If the other person is not committed, it is not really a relationship at all.

Preventing it from lingering on

Once a relationship is over, it can be difficult for both parties to cease contact totally. If children are involved, it is impossible. The person who has been left will have many questions they want answered. They will probably want to win their partner back at any cost. Their emotions are raw and their thinking isn't very clear. They tend to believe that any contact is better than no contact.

The one who left the relationship might want to alleviate their own guilt by letting their partner down slowly, or by trying to remain *friends*. Maybe they will send an email, or make a telephone call, or invite them to dinner, just to keep in contact. Whatever the details, the end point remains the same – the relationship lingers on. What is needed then is for the relationship to come to a definite halt. If the couple has children, then the relationship needs to be redefined so that only the parental relationship continues.

When a relationship has ended, close the door firmly.

What we often see is the hurt experienced by people who are tangled in a lingering relationship. There will of course be great sadness and loneliness when a relationship ends, but allowing it to linger makes it many times worse. At the heart of a lingering relationship are poorly defined boundaries. The relationship, on one hand, is officially over. But on the other hand, the behaviour of the couple suggests otherwise. Being in limbo is worse than the actual pain of breaking up. If there are reasons to end the relationship, delaying the inevitable will not ease the pain. Consider Rosemary's story.

Rosemary's story (25 years)

Rosemary could hardly hold back the tears as she told of why she had come. Her boyfriend Jason had ended their relationship a few months earlier and she was having a really tough time moving on. As her story unfolded, it was not surprising that she was finding it difficult. They still had regular phone contact, they still went out occasionally but, most damaging for Rosemary, they were still having sex.

So at what point do they draw the line and say they are no longer having a relationship? The sad part is that Rosemary believed that seeing Jason on his terms might get their relationship back on track. But when prodded, Rosemary could see that this so-called strategy of hers to 'win Jason back' was failing dismally.

> Every time we go out, we end up sleeping together. It's getting harder and harder; I'm crushed each time because the reality is that nothing changes. I leave hating myself and feeling guilty about what I have done. Jason ends up having a good night's sleep and is still 'free' of me the next day to find himself.

Before she could begin to move on, Rosemary had to see that Jason was having his needs met at her expense; he was having his cake and eating it too. He didn't have time to experience his life without Rosemary. Now, that is not to say there was anything malicious about Jason's behaviour. But he was being selfish. He wanted to keep up the contact with Rosemary and could not understand why in the end she started pulling back. He did not, and could not, understand how much it hurt Rosemary to keep seeing him, hoping that he would change his mind.

During the course of counselling, Rosemary tried to set different limits with Jason. Rosemary also needed to know that she was going through a grieving process; she had to learn to live without Jason in her life. In the end, she told Jason that it was not good for her to keep seeing him like this and she would prefer it if he did not contact her. She, in time, would contact him.

She spent more time during the early days with her own friends. She kept busy at work, started back at the gym and turned her thinking around. Initially she thought: *I'll do anything to get him back.* In time she changed this to: *I don't want to be in a relationship with someone who doesn't want me. If we're meant to be together, it'll happen. If not, I'll have moved on and be in a totally different place in my life.*

Actions speak louder than words

A common trap into which many people fall is to be all talk and no action when it comes to ending a relationship. By meeting your ex-partner to discuss **how** you will be ceasing contact after you've already broken up only sets you both up for further pain. Constant discussions on why a relationship has ended, or why you need to cease contact tend to confuse matters more. Of course, you'd like to understand why someone is ending a relationship with you, but in the long run, revisiting the issue over and over only increases the heartache.

Taking control

When one person ends a relationship, there is a power imbalance favouring the partner who has ended the relationship. It is important for the partner who has been left to take control and set limits. We refer to this as 'keeping the ball in your court'. At first it is hard to do, as it goes against the result you might be striving for – namely, resuming the relationship.

So, if you are the one who has been left, the following guidelines – 'Keeping the ball in your court' – might get you back on track as a person in your own right. But don't expect that you'll be able to do all these things immediately. It takes time and, in a sense, you need to work up to them. Remember that it is totally normal to feel miserable. Allow yourself time to grieve and resist making any major decisions during this stage.

Initially, you might think these guidelines make sense but you doubt your ability to stick to them. That's okay. In our experience, people can have many false starts before they actually put the guidelines in place. Often they have to hit rock bottom before they can move forward in this way. If you feel you are at rock bottom, it is important to ride out the emotion, even if it is very painful. What you need in the early days is support from friends and family, and routine. While all you might want is your partner back, you are likely to only remember their good points and, in a sense, idolise them. This doesn't help you in the long run. What will help is establishing a new life for yourself as a single person.

As you work your way down the list of our suggestions for keeping the ball in your court, you will see that some are designed to help you distance yourself from your partner, while others target ways to help you move on. They all help you try to get some control back in your life. When we suggest exercise and socialising many people say that they just don't feel like it. Although we understand such apathy or reluctance, the sooner you start going through the motions, the easier it will become. We expect there to be a lag in time before your feelings match your behaviour, so don't wait until you feel like doing something, just do it anyway. What gets people through any grieving period is not time itself, but *what you do in the time*. Remember, when grieving there is little room for any other emotion. So, be patient and realistic about how quickly you expect to feel 'better'.

> **It's not time that heals the pain, it is what you do in the time.**

Keeping the ball in your court

- Decide how much contact with your ex you want. (Ideally a complete break of six months helps. Obviously, if children are involved, this is not possible.)
- Don't act impulsively if your ex-partner contacts you.
- Say 'no' to sex.

- List what you believe were the strengths and weaknesses in the relationship to prevent yourself from idolising your ex-partner.
- Think about the consequences of getting back together without resolving the issues?
- Stick to a routine.
- Keep busy with your own activities.
- Exercise.
- Develop new friendships.
- Develop new interests.
- Resist the urge to ask mutual friends for details about your ex's movements.
- Gradually reduce the time spent talking about your ex-partner.
- Gradually reduce the number of friends you talk to about the break-up.
- Resist beginning a new relationship.
- Use clear thinking to change the thoughts that keep you 'stuck'.
- Seek appropriate legal or financial advice.

When a break-up is recent, probably all you will want to do – besides seeing your ex-partner – is to talk over and over what has happened with people close to you. Again, this is a normal response to coping with the loss. In time, you will talk about it less and less. It usually helps, however, to deliberately choose not to talk about your situation at times. Some people may be able to do this one month after the break-up, but for others it may take many more months. We ask our clients to gradually reduce the number of times and the extent to which they discuss their break-up, so that they can focus on the here and now. Similarly, it helps to make the break clearer if you resist asking friends about the movements of your ex-partner. Their activities are no longer your business, just as your movements are none of theirs. Knowing what they are up to or whom they are seeing only prolongs the agony.

> After nine years of a committed relationship, my partner announced that our relationship was over. She doesn't want to be with me anymore. According to her, it was as simple as that. I was devastated. Sure I thought we were going through a rough patch, but not for a moment did I suspect she wanted out. From that announcement on, she wanted things done her way. She wanted us to split our possessions immediately, and sell our unit. I was still in shock. What I learnt to do was keep the ball in my court. I did things in my time. I sought advice from the appropriate people and did not react to her demands. Even though it hurt like hell, one year later I'm moving on.
>
> Jack, 44 years

I don't seem to be getting any better

When we work with people who have been left by their partner, they often need lots of help to adjust to the loss of their partner and relationship. The range and intensity of emotion is great. What can sometimes prevent you from feeling better after a break-up is the tendency for the person who has broken off the relationship to show no remorse. If communication between the two of you continues, your ex-partner can often manage to rub salt into the wound by being increasingly critical of you and your relationship. They might start to rubbish and minimise the entire relationship with statements such as: *We never had a good relationship. I could never talk to you. I have been unhappy for a long time.* It is easy to start believing what you are being told, and therefore to continue to feel miserable. It is very important to try to ignore these statements. Keep away from one another for a period of at least six months (if possible).

Another strategy that we find works is to ask our clients to **write a letter** to their ex-partner telling them whatever is on their mind. But we ask them not to post it. The rationale behind this is to help shift their emotions. They might feel intense sadness, resentment and anger, all at once. Writing it down takes more cognitive effort, and the process alone is very helpful. In a similar way, **keeping a journal** of your thoughts and feelings can also be of great help. In time, as your life gets busier and your focus is on other things, you will write less often.

Helping yourself to move on
- What would you like to be able to say to your ex-partner?
- Write a letter that you don't send. Write as much as you can and then read over it in a few days' time. Have you overlooked anything?

If you want your partner back, you probably realise that the longer it has been, the less likely it is that you'll get back together. Nonetheless, it is often hard to shake your memory of your relationship, and your desire for reconciliation. Look at the following diagram and see what sort of hold your old relationship can have over you.

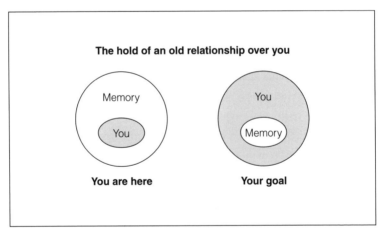

The circle on the left-hand side shows that your memory of the relationship is overshadowing your life. It has control over you and is preventing you from moving on. In the circle on the right, on the other hand, you are in control of your life and the memory of the relationship is just a small part of that.

Obviously the aim is to shift the balance of power, from the memory of the relationship consuming you to the memory of the relationship being only a part of you, using the strategies outlined in 'Keeping the ball in your court' (p. 189).

Of course this might be difficult. If you believe what we are saying, but still live in hope, then it might help you to think about how much longer you want to go on waiting and hoping for your partner to come back. We suggest that you *draw a line*. By that we mean in your own mind set a date towards which you can work. If your partner has not returned by that date, then you can be fairly sure they are not coming back. As this date approaches, it will help, no matter what the outcome, if you follow the strategies listed in 'Keeping the ball in your court'.

One of the most important questions you can ask yourself to help get you back in control is: *Do you want to be with someone who doesn't want to be with you?* Remember what we said earlier: healthy relationships involve two people walking the same path, side by side, not leaning on each other or pulling the other along. This is where looking at your thinking is important. Make sure that your thoughts promote a healthy sense of who you are.

> **The expectation that breaking up will not hurt is unrealistic. The pain does not necessarily mean that the decision is wrong.**

We believe that it is unhealthy to collect ex-partners as friends. Closing the door firmly on relationships allows you to keep the slate clean. Without a clean slate, it is much harder to begin a new relationship.

How to choose a new partner

Before you enter into a new relationship, whether you are the one who left or the one who was left, we recommend the following ground rules. Either way, you have to do some work on yourself to prevent yourself from making the same mistakes again. Many people find this stage very difficult because they believe that they will only feel better if they are being loved or are in love again.

Ground rules for starting a new relationship

- Take a long break.
- Seek counselling if necessary.
- Make friends with the opposite sex.
- Date different people.
- Take it slowly.
- Don't rush into sex.
- Tell yourself that it is okay to be single for a while.

Let's take a closer look at these ground rules. The reason we so strongly advise having a long break is to allow yourself time to process what went wrong. Take the opportunity to build new *friendships*, especially with the opposite sex. By all means see other people, but don't get hooked into another relationship too soon. Otherwise, before you know it, you'll be off in the bubble of new love again. Then you won't have any time or desire to work out what you need to change. No doubt the same old issues will raise their ugly heads at some stage in the new relationship – when exactly, no-one knows.

If you do happen to meet someone sooner than expected, take it slowly and don't immediately rush into a sexual relationship. Once you've passed certain milestones in a relationship, that's it – they can never be recaptured again. If you believe you can't put on the brakes in a new relationship, then try and put some safeguards in place. Not seeing each other every day is a good start. Keep yourself busy with other friends and activities. If you have children, don't introduce new partners to them too soon, even if you think 'this is it', because it is too early to tell. Remember, what builds fast usually breaks fast. Ideally, tell yourself that it is actually good for you not to be in a relationship for a while. Use it as an opportunity to do things that you have been unable to do. Maybe it's a course or a sport you've thought about for ages, or simply making more of an effort with friends and family. If you have children, try to develop new interests with them.

When to choose?

> *Because I have been hurt a number of times, I wait now until their actions match their words before I let myself fall for them.*
>
> Georgina, 36 years

Eventually, you will probably meet someone else. Once you are clear about the reasons why your last relationship didn't work, then you are in a much better place to begin a new one. Of course, there is no guarantee that your new partner will turn out to be any better than your ex-partner. But if you have followed the guidelines in this chapter, have considered the factors listed in 'When to make a commitment' in Chapter 3, and have spent some time looking after your own needs, then take the plunge.

Protecting your new relationship

Because we believe in a preventive approach, we think it is useful to look at how to protect your new relationship, even if you are currently very happy. Believe it or not, the bubble of new love in this new relationship will also pop. Once again, you will then have to carry on the relationship in the context of the rest of your life. By all means enjoy the bubble, but remember its purpose is to protect the developing relationship. Do not think that this is the reality of this new love. It is only the first stage. By not *expecting* the bubble to be there forever, you won't panic when it bursts – as it did before.

IN BRIEF...

- @ It's difficult to move on unless you resolve the reasons why your past relationship failed.
- @ Try not to become a victim.
- @ Don't let a broken relationship linger on.
- @ What you need when a relationship ends are friends – not a new lover.

The lighter side......

Yet another little gem from the Internet (source unknown).

How to impress a woman:
Compliment her.
Respect her.
Honour her.
Cuddle her.
Kiss her.
Caress her.
Love her.
Stroke her.
Tease her.
Comfort her.
Protect her.
Hug her.
Hold her.
Spend money on her.
Wine and dine her.
Buy things for her.
Listen to her.
Care for her.
Stand by her.
Support her.
Go to the ends of the earth for her.

How to impress a man:
Show up naked,
bring beer.

How to enjoy your relationship

We wanted to finish the book on a positive note – and explore ways which might enable you to enjoy your relationship more. As we said in the beginning, our aim is to help couples walk side by side along the same path. To do this requires commitment from both people. Commitment provides the incentive for dealing with the obstacles that get in the way of enjoying a happy relationship. We have outlined a number of techniques to help you rise above some of the down sides of being in a relationship. These techniques have included: the changing of unhelpful thinking patterns, the adjustment of expectations, how to develop yourself as an individual, how to communicate more effectively, and how to take responsibility for the things

you need to change. We have also suggested ways to move on after the end of an unhappy relationship. Now we want to explore strategies that will help you focus on the positives in your relationship.

Strategies to improve your relationship

In order to develop a successful relationship, you and your partner must be prepared to put in the necessary hard work. We don't believe great relationships just happen. They have to be cultivated and nurtured. We believe it is invaluable to set goals as a couple and as individuals. Forget New Year's resolutions. They have their roots in wishful thinking. Rather, focus your attention on your relationship and what's realistic.

Yearly goals

Our 'Yearly goals exercise' asks you to do just that – set goals. You will notice there are three sections. The first section is for each of you to complete individually. We believe your own goals are just as important as your goals as a couple because they help you maintain who you are. The second section is for planning your mutual goals, and the third section asks about the highlights in your relationship during the last year. The third section is really important because, too often in relationships, people get caught in the trap of focusing their attention only on the negative aspects and failing to attend to all the good things. Many of the good times go unnoticed. We recommend that you use a special book for this exercise. Write down your goals at the beginning of each year and the highlights from the year before. By using the same book each year, you can chart your progress. You are also recording some of your history as a couple.

Yearly goals exercise

Section 1: Complete the following questions separately.

1. As an individual, what would you like to achieve in the next twelve months? Be specific, and consider the following areas:
   - friendships
   - leisure activities
   - fitness
   - career/education
   - finances
   - family (extended)
   - children (if applicable)
   - other

2. What steps do you need to take to achieve your goals?

Section 2: Complete the following questions as a couple. Try to agree on the goals.

3. As a couple, what common goals would you like to achieve within the next twelve months? Be as specific as you can, and consider the following areas in your lives:
   - friendships
   - family (extended)
   - sexual relationship
   - children (if any)
   - leisure activities
   - holidays
   - home
   - finances
   - time spent together
   - other

4. What steps do you need to take to achieve your goals?
5. Decide together which area you want to target first, second, and so on.

Section 3: Complete this question as a couple.

6. Think back over the past year. What events were the highlights of the year? They might include the birth of a child, a fabulous holiday together, or a time when you really worked well as a team. Write a description of what happened, where you were and what made it so special.

Marianne and Pete's story

Marianne: *Well first and foremost we love each other. My darling and I have been very happily married for 34 years. It's hard to say why it still works – it might sound corny but I think it's because, apart from love, we have respect for each other. I like to treat my darling as the most important 'guest' in our home, but I don't devalue myself either. I enjoy my wine in crystal, so that's how I drink it.*

No matter what happens, I like to use the old Jewish saying which is, 'If this is the worst thing that happens in your life, it's a sweet life ahead'. I try to put things into perspective, in other words, how important is it?

We also are not into 'point scoring'. I notice that a lot with other couples and I think it belittles them and the marriage.

Pete: *My own mother and father's marriage was not too flash, so when I met Marianne's parents and saw how a good marriage works, it was easy for me to pick up on their positive relationship. Early in the piece Marianne's dad said to me that, 'Marriage is to give all and expect nothing in return!' I have practised this statement for 34 years, and it works.*

Twenty-odd years ago, when discussing an impending partnership arrangement at work, the accountant said that, 'A good partnership is like a good marriage without the sex!' What comes around, goes around.

I think it is really important to have a sense of humour, it can lighten up a serious situation and remove the conversational blocks that take place when anger is in the voice.

At least one person in a successful marriage must be patient. Patience creates the ability to listen, listening forces you to understand. If you don't understand exactly what is being said, you must ask for more information to clarify what is being said, or meant. This is really important.

Focus on the positives

Remember the aim is to work towards focusing more on the positive aspects of being in a relationship and less on the negative parts. When couples hit a stale patch, they often forget what attracted them to their partner in the first place, how they felt in those early days, and what fun things they used to do together. It's important to remember that these experiences each contribute something different to create your own unique relationship path that distinguishes your relationship from anyone else's.

She was fun to be with, attractive and had a very easy-going personality.

Grahame, 34 years

I loved the fact that he was always full of life. He was motivated and energetic. Nothing was ever too difficult.

Ellen, 36 years

I was first attracted to his friendly and kind personality and his self-confidence.

Nance, 33 years

He is older and so he appeared more mature than males my own age. Not bad looking either.

Carole, 35 years

Even though at times we get on each other's nerves, when he's been away for a while I really miss him, and some of those feelings from our early days together come bouncing back.

Katherine, 33 years

What's your couple story?

Think back to when you first met. What attracted you to your partner? What things did you enjoy together? How did you feel?

Write these answers down so you can keep them in mind, especially at times when you might question your relationship.

> *We used to spend a lot of time outdoors and travelling to new places. We certainly shared some great experiences.*
>
> Clare, 32 years

Josie's story

Martin and I have been together for eighteen years — married for fifteen years, and have a beautiful nineteen-month-old son. We began our relationship when we were 21 during our final year at university. Prior to this we were good friends, originally meeting in year 11 at high school. In retrospect it seems so young to connect with someone who will become your life partner but it felt so right from the very beginning.

There are a number of features in our relationship that have always been present and that I think make it successful. Martin is my closest friend and I love being with him and want to spend as much time as possible with him. We have very similar values, goals and interests, and while we are definitely not clones of each other, having a lot in common has certainly contributed to making our relationship very stable. We feel very much a team.

Our relationship has an ease about it and it flows very smoothly. I have always been able to be myself, warts and all! Martin and I enjoy each other's sense of humour and have shared a lot of laughter and fun.

In the early years of our relationship we made some very deliberate decisions that we try to abide by. These include finding a balance between our home and working lives that feels comfortable for both of us and resolving disagreements quickly and not dwelling on them. We are fortunate in that we have few arguments and, to date, have never carried an argument over to the next day.

Last but not least, I feel so very lucky to be sharing my life with Martin who is such a loving and caring person. He is devoted to me and makes me feel very special. Marrying him was the best decision of my life.

Martin's story

For me entering into a lifelong relationship was not a difficult decision. I had known Josie as a friend since school days and if I am honest I always thought that she was too good for me and wouldn't be interested. I was wrong, not about her being too good because she is almost too good to be true, but when circumstance brought us closer together she was interested and we quickly fell in love. I knew very early on in our relationship that I wanted to share my entire life with her and this feeling is as strong today as it was twenty years ago.

Our marriage so far has been very successful and it is hard sometimes to understand why so many others have not survived. Clearly the compatibility of our personalities and our personal values is a big part of it. We are both fairly rational, gentle and caring and calm people who enjoy life and try to keep a balanced view. We have a deep respect for each other and really work as a team. I couldn't imagine life without my darling wife, I would be like a fish out of water. We always make decisions together, we know each other's skills and weaknesses and together we can get so much more out of life than we could on our own.

I sometimes look at people who have been in marriages of 50 or 60 years, who clearly have a good, strong almost symbiotic relationship, and think of all the change that they have seen in their lives: from newlyweds to great-grandparents, the different phases that they have been through, inevitably some good times and bad and inevitably sickness and health. I hope that one day I will be in their position and can look back and say it was that intangible thing 'love' that bound us together on this journey and made our relationship a successful marriage. For me being a good husband and father is what really counts in life.

Keep a record

We also believe that it is a good exercise to write down some of the enjoyable or memorable moments in your life as a couple. Those of you with children are no doubt pretty good at taking photos or videos of them to show them when they are older. As in the third section in the 'Yearly goals exercise', we recommend that you record really special moments. It could be something relatively simple, such as when you felt a strong connection with your partner, or you could write a brief paragraph to accompany a photo. Collecting significant keepsakes such as cards is another suggestion. They're all great ways to record your own history. Women are more likely to want to do this. That's okay, but if at least you encourage your men to contribute to your yearly goals, you're on the right track. Perhaps a nice meal and a bottle of wine will entice them?

Celebrate everything

Remember when you were younger. At a gathering with friends, someone would get up and make a toast to something. The more you celebrated, the more you wanted to toast. Now, you need to celebrate and congratulate each other on small and large achievements – another year, a pay rise, a successful dinner party. Being mindful of the little things helps to keep the focus on the positives.

We believe it's important to resist the urge to care less and less about special dates such as birthdays and anniversaries. On the contrary, we encourage couples to celebrate more and more. You don't have to exchange lavish gifts to celebrate such events. It's more about reinforcing the fact that your relationship and your partner are special.

Aim to bring out the best in each other

Part of working together as a team is helping your partner be the best person they can. If they could conquer further challenges – encourage them! If they do not realise a certain behaviour or way of thinking is hindering their progress – let them know your thoughts. Of course, it is up to your partner whether or not they heed your advice, but at least you are making the suggestions. It would be nice if you were the other person's greatest fan.

How to refocus and prioritise

We can suggest many other strategies to help you focus on the positives in your relationship. One is to keep a record for a week of the time you spend together as a couple. This exercise is useful as it raises your awareness of the patterns in your relationship. Another strategy is to praise the good and ignore the bad. What's important here is that you are making a conscious decision to focus on the positives. Everyone likes to be rewarded, and we know that positive reinforcement actually increases the likelihood of a particular behaviour occurring again. So, when your partner does something you like, tell them so!

Use a calendar
Keep a calendar for one week and record the time you spend together as a couple.

> **When your partner does something you like, don't forget to tell them so.**

With busy schedules, it's also easy to forget that you were once so much in love with your partner that you could barely wait to see them. That was your bubble phase, you say. You are now in the mature phase of your relationship, when the urgency and desire to be with each other has been overshadowed by the repetition and chaos of daily living. While it's perfectly normal for outside events to take you away from your partner some of the time, it is crucial to regard each other as your number one priority. Don't fall into the trap of complacency, expecting that your partner will always be waiting.

Another suggestion for helping you keep your relationship a priority include: a surprise night out with your partner. It doesn't have to be expensive to be fun; it is certainly the thought that counts. Similarly, saying 'I love you', or ringing your partner unexpectedly to let them know you were thinking about them, can send a strong message. Get into the habit of setting aside a small amount of time on weekends just to be with each other. It might only be for a cup of tea but, nonetheless, it sends an important message, especially to children, that *your relationship is valuable*. It also provides an opportunity for having a regular update on what's happening.

Having a good understanding or knowledge of what your partner does during the working week, whether it be at home or at work, keeps you focused on each other. Being able to describe in public, for example, what your partner does can mean a lot as it reflects the time and energy you have put into finding out in the first place. Following up on past discussions about the week, such as important meetings or activities with children, all send messages that your partner is important to you. Talking positively about your partner to other people, especially when they are not there, helps to remind you of their positive qualities and how wonderful they are. It also keeps you aware of the fact that you are a team.

Some general tips

We hope that, by using the strategies in this book, you'll be on the path to a happy relationship. Our 'Successful relationship "Do" list' below summarises the strategies we believe are important.

Successful relationship 'Do' list

- See yourself as a team.
- Be mindful of your partner's needs.
- Complete the 'Yearly goals exercise'.
- Plan sexual interludes, especially after you have children.
- Plan regular dates as a couple (even at home).
- Spend time away from your main family or friend network if the opportunity arises (e.g. living interstate or overseas) as it can strengthen the relationship.
- Make sure you tell your partner important things before you tell anyone else.
- Don't discuss your private problems with everyone.
- Maintain loyalty to your partner at all times.
- Adopt an attitude of 'going with the flow'.
- Pick your fights.
- Accept your partner, warts and all.
- Keep your thinking realistic.
- Rise to the challenge of improving your relationship at all times.
- Aim to go to bed at the same time most nights, if possible.

We asked some older people, who had enjoyed successful relationships, what they thought was important in having a good relationship and what their advice to new couples starting out would be. This is what a few of them had to say.

Work things out, talk things over, try to have common goals and don't worry about the trivialities.

Stephanie, 63 years

Remember you should be each other's best friend.

Mary, 60

Be prepared to make sacrifices as far as your present lifestyle goes.

Stewart, 60 years

Be supportive of each other, communicate and make sure you find the time in your busy lives to be just the two of you again.

Lillian, 71 years

I think being able to give and take is very important.

Gwen, 60 years

So, at the end of your life, it would be nice to be able to sit back and be proud of yourself for what you have achieved in your relationship. We doubt if many of you will want to remember the times that he didn't do this, or she didn't do that. Rather, what will count will be how the two of you negotiated your relationship path, and the experiences you shared along the way.

We have always tried to make time for our mutual interests apart from our kids.

Tony, 65 years

Acknowledgements

We'd like to thank the many individuals and couples who answered our questionnaires, told us their stories, and gave us their photos.

Rex Finch guided us once again throughout the conception, editing and design phases of the book. Along with Vicki, Sarah, and Meg, this book was definitely a team effort – thank you.

We would also like to thank our families and friends. In particular, thank you to Andrew and David for being there for us and providing us with our own experiences of a committed relationship.

Finally, we want to thank our parents. They were our role models and continue to be our inspiration.

Jo Lamble and Sue Morris

What is a clinical psychologist?

Clinical psychologists help people identify and change unhelpful behaviours and thinking patterns. They use a variety of techniques including interviews, observation and tests. There are many treatment approaches and techniques from which a clinical psychologist will select, according to the presenting problem.

Clinical psychologists are specialist psychologists with a minimum of six years' full-time university training. All practising psychologists must be registered with their State or Territory Registration Board.

Clinical psychologists help prevent, assess, diagnose and treat a wide range of problems encountered by children, adolescents and adults. Common areas of treatment include alcohol and drug problems, anxiety disorders, behavioural difficulties, chronic pain, depression, eating disorders, grief, relationship difficulties, trauma reactions and stress.

For more information about where to find a clinical psychologist, contact the Australian Psychological Society or the New Zealand College of Clinical Psychologists.

Further reading

Andrews, G., Crino, R., Hunt, C., Lampe, L., and Page, A., *The Treatment of Anxiety Disorders*, Cambridge University Press, Melbourne, 1994.

Ballinger, S. and Walker, W. L., *Not the Change of Life; Breaking the menopause taboo*, Penguin Books, Victoria, 1987.

Beck, A.T., *Cognitive Therapy and the Emotional Disorders*, International Universities Press, New York, 1976.

Beiber, J., *If Divorce Is the Only Way*, Penguin Books, Victoria, 1998.

Biddulph, S., *Manhood: An action plan for changing men's lives*, Finch Publishing, Sydney, 1994.

Burns, D., *Feeling Good: The new mood therapy*, Information Australia Group, Melbourne, 1980.

Catalino, E., *The Chronic Pain Control Workbook*, New Harbinger Publications, California, 1997.

Ellis, A. and Harper, R.A., *A New Guide to Rational Living*, Wilshire Book Company, Hollywood, 1975.

Fisher, B., *Rebuilding: When your relationship ends*, Impact Publishers, California, 1998.

Green, M., *Fathers After Divorce*, Finch Publishing, Sydney, 1998.

Green, T., *If You Really Loved Me...The no-nonsense, how-to-get-a-life guide to relationships*, Random House Australia, Sydney, 1996.

Green, Toby, *The Men's Room: A thinking man's guide for surviving women of the next millennium*, Random House, Sydney, 1999.

Greenberger, D. and Padesky, C., *Mind Over Mood; Change how you feel by changing the way you think*, Guildford Press, New York, 1995.

King, Rosie, *Good Loving, Great Sex: Finding balance when your sex drives differ*, Random House, Sydney, 1997.

Lamble, J. and Morris, S., *Motherhood, Making it work for you*, Finch publishing, Sydney, 1999.

McKissock, M., *Coping with Grief*, Australian Broadcasting Corporation, Sydney, 1985.

Mellor, K. & E., *Parentcraft*, Finch Publishing, Sydney, 1999.

Montgomery, B. and Evans, L., *Living and Loving Together*, Penguin, Melbourne, 1995.

Montgomery, B. and Evans, L., *You & Stress*, Viking O'Neill, Melbourne, 1984.

Page, A., *Don't Panic! Overcoming anxiety, phobias and tension*, Health Books, Sydney, 1993.

Pudney, W. and Cotterell, J., *Beginning Fatherhood: A guide for expectant fathers*, Finch Publishing, Sydney, 1998.

Rapee, R., *Overcoming Shyness and Social Phobia*, Lifestyle Press, Sydney, 1998.

Tanner, S. and Ball, J., *Beating the Blues*, Self-published, Sydney, 1999.

Notes

Page vi **Cognitive Behaviour Therapy**
Beck, A.T., *Cognitive Therapy and the Emotional Disorders*, International Universities Press, New York, 1976.
Ellis, A. and Harper, R.A., *A New Guide to Rational Living*, Wilshire Book Company, Hollywood, 1975.

Page 3 **Commitment**
For further reading on commitment, see Green, Toby, *If You Really Loved Me...The no-nonsense, how-to-get-a-life guide to relationships*, Random House Australia, Sydney, 1996.
King, Rosie, *Good Loving, Great Sex: Finding balance when your sex drives differ*, Random House, Sydney, 1997.

Page 11 **Two people becoming as one**
This idea is mentioned in Fisher, B., *Rebuilding: When your relationship ends*, Impact Publishers, California, 1998.

Page 37 **Teenagers' expectations**
A number of year 11 and 12 students kindly answered a questionnaire which asked about their expectations of successful relationships.

Page 38 **Children change the course**
For a very detailed discussion on the effects of children on relationships, see Lamble, J. and Morris, S., *Motherhood: Making it work for you*, Finch Publishing, Sydney, 1999.

Page 45 **Domestic IQ**
This interesting term was introduced to us by Filomena Leonardi.

Page 64 **Clear thinking**
The framework outlined in Chapter 6 is based on the psychological model known as Cognitive Behaviour Therapy (CBT). For a more in-depth discussion of CBT, see Ellis, A. and Harper, R.A., *A New Guide to Rational Living*, Wilshire Book Company, Hollywood, 1975.

Page 67 **Common inaccurate assumptions about relationships**
For a more in-depth discussion about the common myths about relationships, see Montgomery, B. and Evans, L., *Living and Loving Together*, Penguin, Melbourne, 1995.

Page 71 **Questions used to challenge your unhelpful thinking**
These questions are based on discussions found in Greenberger, D. and Padesky, C., *Mind Over Mood; Change how you feel by changing the way you think*, Guildford Press, New York, 1995; and Andrews, G., Crino, R., Hunt, C., Lampe, L., and Page, A., *The Treatment of Anxiety Disorders*, Cambridge University Press, Melbourne, 1994.

Page 74 **Faulty thinking**
Further examples are discussed in Tanner, S. and Ball, J., *Beating the Blues*, Self-published, Sydney, 1999.

Page 83 **Life events stress**
For a more detailed discussion of how life events affect wellbeing, see Montgomery, B. and Evans, L., *You & Stress*, Viking O'Neill, Melbourne, 1984.

Page 109 **Jealousy**
A further discussion can be found in Tanner, S. and Ball, J., *Beating the Blues,* Self-published, Sydney, 1999.

Page 113 **Thinking clearly about sex**
A very helpful look at sexual relationships can be found in King, Rosie, *Good Loving, Great Sex: Finding balance when your sex drives differ,* Random House, Sydney, 1997.

Page 122 **Framework for making choices**
Further reading on problem solving can be found in Montgomery, B. and Evans, L., *You & Stress,* Viking O'Neill, Melbourne, 1984.

Page 128 **Wedding vows**
These five lines are taken from The Uniting Church of Australia, *Uniting in Worship,* Uniting Education, Victoria, 1998.

Page 130 **Parenthood**
Valuable reading on parenthood includes: Biddulph, S., *Manhood: An action plan for changing men's lives,* Finch Publishing, Sydney, 1994; Lamble, J. and Morris, S., *Motherhood: Making it work for you,* Finch Publishing, Sydney, 1999; Mellor, K. and E., *Parentcraft,* Finch Publishing, Sydney, 1999; Pudney, W. and Cotterell, J., *Beginning Fatherhood: A guide for expectant fathers,* Finch Publishing, Sydney, 1998.

Page 144 **Menopause**
For a useful discussion on menopause, see Ballinger, S. and Walker, W.-L., *Not the Change of Life: Breaking the menopause taboo,* Penguin Books, Victoria, 1987.

Page 145 **Depression**
An excellent book on depression is Tanner, S. and Ball, J., *Beating the Blues,* Self-published, Sydney, 1999.

Page 145 **Anxiety**
Two worthwhile references for anxiety are Rapee, R., *Overcoming Shyness and Social Phobia,* Lifestyle Press, Sydney, 1998; and Page, A., *Don't Panic! Overcoming anxiety, phobias and tension,* Health Books, Sydney, 1993.

Page 146 **Grief**
For an excellent book on grief, see McKissock, M., *Coping with Grief,* Australian Broadcasting Corporation, Sydney, 1985.

Page 149 **Affairs**
Toby Green's books include useful discussions on affairs. Green, T., *If You Really Loved Me...The no-nonsense, how-to-get-a-life guide to relationships,* Random House Australia, Sydney, 1996; and Green, T., *The Men's Room: A thinking man's guide for surviving women of the next millennium,* Random House, Sydney, 1999.

Page 165 **Divorce**
A helpful discussion on a difficult subject can be found in Beiber, J., *If Divorce Is the Only Way,* Penguin Books, Victoria, 1998.

Page 176 **What now?**
For further reading on how to rebuild your life after an affair, see Fisher, B., *Rebuilding: When your relationship ends,* Impact Publishers, California, 1998.

Page 197 **Happy relationships**
Some helpful hints on how to make your relationship more rewarding can be found in Montgomery, B. and Evans, L., *Living and Loving Together,* Penguin, Melbourne, 1995.

Cognitive Diary

| Date/Time | Situation | Thoughts | Feelings/Behaviour | New thoughts | New feelings/Behaviour |
	A	B	C	D	E

Index

Finch titles

Beginning Fatherhood
A guide for expectant fathers
Warwick Pudney and Judy Cottrell
ISBN 1876451017

The Body Snatchers
How the media shapes women
Cyndi Tebbel
ISBN 1876451076

Boys in Schools
Addressing the real issues – behaviour, values and relationships
Rollo Browne and Richard Fletcher
ISBN 0646239589

Bullybusting
How to help children deal with teasing and bullying
Evelyn Field
ISBN 1876451041

Dealing with Anger
Self-help solutions for men
Frank Donovan
ISBN 187645105X

Fathers After Divorce
Building a new life and becoming a successful separated parent
Michael Green
ISBN 1876451009

Fathers, Sons and Lovers
Men talk about their lives from 1930s to today
Dr Peter West
ISBN 0646288164

Girls' Talk
Young women speak their hearts and minds
Maria Palotta-Chiarolli
ISBN 1876451025

Manhood
An action plan for changing men's lives
Steve Biddulph
ISBN 0646261444

Motherhood
Making it work for you
Jo Lamble and Sue Morris
ISBN 1876451033

On Their Own
Boys growing up underfathered
Rex McCann
ISBN 1876451092

Parentcraft
Essential skills for raising children from infancy to adulthood
Ken and Elizabeth Mellor
ISBN 1876451068

Raising Boys
Why boys are different – and how to help them become happy and well-balanced men
Steve Biddulph
ISBN 0646314181

Finch titles are available in bookshops or at www.finch.com.au